WRITE YOUR STRESS AWAY

WRITE YOUR STRESS AWAY

Tame the Tension in Your Life

**Diane Hartingh Price and
Susan Ives McCollum**

ROWMAN & LITTLEFIELD
Lanham • Boulder • New York • London

Published by Rowman & Littlefield
An imprint of The Rowman & Littlefield Publishing Group, Inc.
4501 Forbes Boulevard, Suite 200, Lanham, Maryland 20706
www.rowman.com

6 Tinworth Street, London SE11 5AL

British Library Cataloguing in Publication Information Available

Library of Congress Cataloging-in-Publication Data

Names: Price, Diane Hartingh, 1949– author. | McCollum, Susan Ives, 1946– author.
Title: Write your stress away : tame the tension in your life / Diane Hartingh Price and Susan Ives McCollum.
Description: Lanham, MD : Rowman & Littlefield, [2019] | Includes bibliographical references and index.
Identifiers: LCCN 2018060859 (print) | LCCN 2019000427 (ebook) | ISBN 9781538117996 (electronic) | ISBN 9781538117989 (cloth : alk. paper)
Subjects: Stress (Psychology) | Emotions. | Self-actualization (Psychology) | Stress management.
Classification: LCC BF575.S75 (ebook) | LCC BF575.S75 P745 2019 (print) | DDC 155.9/042—dc23
LC record available at https://lccn.loc.gov/2018060859

For all people in the world, may they find peace, wellness, and healing from stress. Write on!

CONTENTS

CONTENTS

INTRODUCTION

How Writing Changed Our Lives

Our story begins with two young women pushing baby strollers up and down the hills of our neighborhood. On our daily walks, our conversation often drifted toward our shared passion for writing, health, and well-being. This led to a lasting friendship based on our common interests in nutrition and exercise, foundations for good health. Fast forward twenty years later when we each were diagnosed with a life-threatening disease—Sue with type 1 diabetes and Diane with breast cancer. In that moment, life changed drastically for both of us. Diane had surgeries and treatment options to make decisions about, side effects to research, insurance calls to make, and a long list of dietary and exercise recommendations to consider. Sue had to learn how to manage a new lifestyle that demanded healthy eating, regular exercise, and close monitoring of blood glucose. We both felt threatened by our diseases, knowing they would change our lives forever. As dramatic as it sounds, this was our new reality!

Although our paths took us in different directions, we both relied on our journal writing to get us through the challenging period after our diagnoses and the stress associated with huge lifestyle changes. When we finally had time to share our experiences, we were struck by how writing had been the lifeline we'd clutched to as we managed our stress through each phase of our healing. We agreed that writing brought us new clarity when we were faced with decisions, reinforced what really mattered most, and offered us a release valve in those moments when we were emotionally overwhelmed.

It became clear that writing was a powerful healing tool for us. Why not introduce it to others as a method to manage stress and implement healthy lifestyle changes? We began sifting through all the research and anecdotal evidence to confirm our belief that writing heals. Our decision to write this book grew out of that research and was again reinforced when we took a writing course at Duke Integrative Medicine together. It was called "Leading Patients in Writing for Health," based on the research and findings of James W. Pennebaker, PhD, and John F. Evans, EdD. Afterward, we sat down and developed a simple writing system based on our experiences and supported by research, using writing to diminish stress and heal mind, body, and spirit. We found, to our great satisfaction, that friends, family, and clients who tried our writing method loved it—and the results it brought. The Write to Be Well method was born out of our personal and professional experiences with writing! But before we go any further, here's a little background on the two of us and how we've used writing to sort out life's challenges.

DIANE'S STORY

Writing things down became a way of life for me at a young age. I was raised in a stiff-upper-lip family where I learned to do whatever needed to be done, sometimes at a high emotional cost. Reflecting on those days, I remember scribbling down my feelings in childish scrawl and then hiding the paper in my little pink suitcase. Little did I know what a gift of healing that would one day become!

Journal writing became a mainstay for me, and I reached for pen and paper intuitively as I navigated through the churning emotional waters of my young life. Wherever I was on the spectrum of life and health, I turned to writing to get in touch with my emotions. Once done, I could always find the clarity to discover what I needed for self-healing.

While on a business trip, I found a lump in my left breast only a few months after a mammogram had told me *all is fine*. Stunned, I sat on the plane home and, with shaking fingers, wrote down all my thoughts. Instinctively, I knew that something was *very* wrong. As I proceeded through the medical tests and doctors' appointments, I insisted on having a biopsy *immediately* rather than waiting another six months. This was *my* life, and I was ready to fight for it!

Throughout those days and weeks, I wrote daily, often several times a day. Just doing so helped me uncover the emotions that caused me to feel like a victim. Instead, I began to focus on becoming a self-advocate. When the biopsy indeed revealed malignancy requiring surgery and chemotherapy, my doctor later remarked that writing had probably saved my life!

In retrospect, though, I believe it was more than that. By writing about what mattered to me in the form of powerful affirmations, I was inspired to *live life fully*. My affirmation, "I live a healthy life, seeing my grandchildren grow well into adulthood," continues to be a beacon for my future each day. As I tackle new changes and evolve by doing so, I continue repeating this pattern of writing: I tell my story, affirm what matters, design a plan and commit to action, and reflect on what I've learned. It's how I successfully manage stress and forge ahead through whatever life throws in my path.

I realized, as time went on, that I wanted to share the gift of writing with others in my professional life. During my years as a vice president in a large consulting firm, I got to know the leaders of various organizations. As we worked together, they began to share their own personal challenges with me, especially their feelings of frustration when they were rebuffed after trying to improve situations within their organizations. These executives paid a huge price—their health—as they dealt with stress.

When I suggested they use writing, they agreed to give it a try and were impressed by the positive change, for both themselves and their staff members. Encouraged, I decided to leave the corporate world after more than twenty-five years to focus on helping others improve their personal and organizational health.

After completing the Duke Integrative Medicine health coach training, my life work now focuses on health, writing, coaching, community service, and consulting. For years, my email closing has been "Be Well!" I mean that wholeheartedly; it's an affirmation and intention rolled into one. It is also central to the process Sue and I want to share so readers can achieve a boost in their physical, mental, and emotional health.

SUE'S STORY

I've always been a writer—an English and journalism major in college, newsletter publisher, grant writer, marketing copywriter, you name it. If it involves words, I love it! I started writing personal narratives in my midtwenties when I was going through a particularly stressful time of life. My journal was my safety valve, holding the secrets to all my emotional turmoil and guiding me through rocky waters.

When I wrote down my thoughts and feelings, I gained the clarity I needed to chart my next course of action. I've always turned to writing at critical junctures in my life. That's why it felt natural to journal about my health crisis when I was diagnosed with diabetes.

On day one, I walked out of the doctor's office with pamphlets listing diabetes dos and don'ts. I was shocked and confused by my diagnosis. I didn't know where to begin, only that I had to adjust my diet, exercise, manage my stress, stick my fingers six to eight times a day, and plan how to handle an emergency if my blood sugar fell too quickly or went too high.

Instinctively, I pulled out my journal and wrote. I had a million questions about diabetes to ask my healthcare providers at my next appointment. I wondered if I could manage this daunting illness on my own. In my journal, I wrote about the grief I felt about losing my good health, and the lifestyle changes required to manage the disease. I expressed my fear that diabetes would kill me if I didn't get it under control immediately! Writing honestly about my feelings about having a chronic disease released my stress and helped me prioritize what I needed to do to thrive with diabetes.

Around the same time I was diagnosed, I began taking classes to become a facilitator in legacy, creative, and memoir writing. I also achieved a master's degree in pastoral counseling, which I combined with my interest in writing, and began leading therapeutic writing groups for my clients and others.

Over time, I witnessed how valuable personal narrative and stories are. I still remember a client who quietly listened to others in our group, never sharing her own writing. One day, I introduced a variety of objects to serve as writing prompts for stories: an empty wine bottle, a child's ballet costume, a broom, a hammer, a seashell. My client surprised me by choosing the broom. When I asked for volunteers to share their stories, she raised her hand and read, "I want to sweep the pain out of my life." That broom was a strong image for her, which led to a bigger story that she shared with us over several more weeks of writing together. Members of this group and those in other groups I've led since told me how much better they felt after writing. Their comments confirmed for me the healing power of writing.

A few years later, I had the opportunity to facilitate writing groups with women living in Malawi, Africa. For many, this was the first time they'd been encouraged to write their stories and express their feelings about events they'd experienced. I heard painful stories of rape and incest, HIV/AIDS, gnawing hunger, and resilience. I witnessed the power of writing to touch deep places within these women and saw what it meant to them to finally share their secrets. Although it was not easy for them to write about their traumas, they felt relieved, affirmed, and, finally, heard.

By sharing their experiences, these women tapped into a deep reservoir of buried pain and emotions. Despite the challenges of confronting those memories, the Malawian women experienced a positive effect, too. The writing released their pent-up emotions and primed them for physical and emotional healing. This experience confirmed for me that writing our life stories, the painful ones as well as the joyful ones, has the potential to heal anyone, in any culture and in any language.

I continue to apply what I've learned about writing to the challenges diabetes demands of me. This unrelenting, inconvenient disease is with me 24/7, but writing about it has helped me shift my perspective so I can live with it successfully, without having it rule my life. The affirmation I live with daily is "I am a healthy, vibrant woman." It reminds me that diabetes is not my whole life story; it is merely one story line among many in my personal narrative. And ultimately, this is true for all of us. We are so much more than any one illness or stress or trauma that might test our physical or emotional well-being. By keeping that truth in perspective, we can focus instead on thriving, not merely surviving!

OUR STORY

Our personal health journeys and our belief that writing heals the stress of physical, emotional, and spiritual pain brought us to this point of creating a brand-new writing method anyone can access, anytime and anywhere. In this book we present Write to Be Well, which is unique in that it sequences four writing steps, building one on the next, to lead you to discover and take action on the changes you desire. The more you use the integrated method, the easier it will be to adapt the four steps to your needs. In the stories our clients share, you'll witness how they've managed their stress and optimized their health with writing; their names have been changed to protect their confidentiality. Use them as role models and then jump right into the writing yourself and learn how Write to Be Well will tame the tension in your life.

Section I

The Journey from Stress to Well-Being

We have always shared a fascination with health and wellness. It began way back when we first met and would sit at the kitchen table and chat about our journeys dedicated to healthy lives for ourselves and our families. Our conversation was sometimes about food, or maybe the value of regular exercise, or the *aha*s in experiencing the mind–body connection. Our shared values were an innate driver preparing us each for futures that were yet to unfold.

Then, too, writing was a persistent part of our lives. We both kept journals and wrote regularly about our life journeys, the thoughts, feelings, and emotions that go with the inevitable changes time brings. Our friendship endured and deepened as we each dealt with the stresses of life: major health challenges; loved ones aging and dying; kids growing up and leaving home; the questions of career, life's purpose, and simply living in our world.

When we committed to writing this book, it was because we wanted to share the lessons of our experience and discoveries about the power of writing and its link to health. We were compelled to dig deeply into the research about stress, health, and writing. We wanted to be sure our facts and experiences were both valid and rock solid before bringing them to you. This solid foundation is the core of our Write to Be Well method.

To that end, this first section lays out the proven foundation of research, theory, and practice. At times the two chapters in this section might sound academic. We've done our best to simply lay out the invaluable discoveries and proof about the negative impact of stress on health and the benefits of writing as an amazing weapon in the war against stress. Please bear with us in this foundational section. We hope you experience some *ahas* as we share the wisdom of the many researchers from the past hundred-plus years. Here's what you will find in Section 1.

Chapter 1 is all about stress, providing a fresh view of the following:

- The types and kinds,
- The difference between stress as a physical threat and its perception,
- How stress impacts your mind, body, and spirit, for better or worse,
- And why today it is a lifestyle disease that is literally killing us.

Chapter 2 is about writing, where we share:

- How anyone can be a writer to effectively manage and ease the impact of stress,
- The research behind the power of writing,
- And the types of writing proven to have measurable benefits to invite better physical, emotional, and mental health.

I

STRESS

Your Hidden Threat

Late on a Friday afternoon, the familiar beep signaling the arrival of a text message rang out on my mobile phone. It was from a longtime friend, Nicole, with whom I'd not spoken in a couple months. The message was succinct. All it said was, "Help! Please call!"

Quickly I called my friend. Within a few minutes she expressed all that was going on in her life. It was a rich mix of her natural enthusiasm for life and the unconscious stressful undercurrent of an ongoing work situation, challenges at home with child-care issues, and feeling saddened by the events reported on the news she was heavily addicted to following. In terms of stress, it was a mix of the good and the bad.

What prompted her to text me was that she had reached a critical tipping point. She had received a voicemail message from her physician's office asking her to call regarding results of her recent mammogram. It was Friday afternoon and too late for her to call back. She thought the worst—cancer. How was she going to make it through the weekend? She knew I'd been through a similar health experience. I was grateful she reached out. When she spoke, she ran through a long list of reasons she couldn't deal with treatment because of her work, family responsibilities, and finances even though she had no facts. She said she felt nauseous and dizzy. She had jumped to the conclusion she had a malignancy, and she simply couldn't handle it. She felt overwhelmed. This was in addition to all the other unconscious stress in her life that was just too much! Do you ever experience the overwhelming feeling of stress?

Stress, we hear about it in the media, from our healthcare providers, and from a variety of sources. The U.S. Centers for Disease Control and Prevention (CDC) reports that 110 million people die every year as a direct result of stress. That is seven people every two seconds. In addition, 75–90 percent of all physician office visits are reported to be for stress-related ailments and complaints. Heart disease, cancer, lung ailments, accidents, cirrhosis of the liver, and suicide are reported as the six leading causes of death, all with proven links to stress. Diabetes is noted as a seventh leading cause of death.[1] How did we get to this startling point?

This chapter explores what stress is and how we have gained the current understanding of its impact on our health and well-being. It lays the foundation for why and how writing can help us deal with stress in our everyday lives. What we have learned about stress and what we've experienced with writing to manage it are the compelling reasons we have written this book.

UNDERSTANDING STRESS

The Science of Physical Threats

At the beginning of the twentieth century, Walter Bradford Cannon was an early researcher in the area of emotion and physiology, or the way living organisms and their parts function.[2] In 1915 he published a groundbreaking book titled *Bodily Changes in Pain, Hunger, Fear and Rage*. Over one hundred years ago, he established the foundation for understanding how our physical bodies react to stress, or a threat, as he described it.[3] Of course, one hundred years ago, *stress* wasn't the household word it is today.

Cannon coined the phrase *fight or flight* based on his initial animal studies showing how the autonomic nervous system releases stress hormones to mobilize a mammal to do just that—fight off a predator or run![4] Since most of us don't walk around knowing some of this medical jargon, here are a few definitions:

- The *autonomic nervous system* is a control system that unconsciously regulates bodily functions, such as heart rate, digestion, and breathing.
- Among *stress hormones* released are adrenaline, noradrenaline, corticosteroid/cortisol, and epinephrine.[5]
- Cannon established how the *sympathetic-adrenal system* facilitates changes in blood supply, blood glucose, and clotting to generate energy to carry out the fight or flight response. This system works in conjunction with the autonomic nervous system described above.

Cannon applied these findings in further research during World War I to better understand ways to treat people who'd experienced the trauma of battle.

From Cannon's early work, we can understand the basic physiology of stress.[6] He defined this as the *stress reaction*, as it is still called today. It's quite simple in that the basic stress reaction built into our bodies supports us in our ability to survive. The many physical reactions support our brain's decision to react to a threat by providing energy, and a mechanism to return our bodies to their natural resting state once the threat is over. This resting state was termed *homeostasis* by Claude Bernard, a French physiologist.[7]

Simply put, Cannon's observations showed that when faced with a physical threat, a mammal's natural reaction was to fight, most likely out of anger or aggression, and the physiological response provided the energy to do so. Similarly, if the reaction to the threat was to flee, most likely out of fear, the same physiological response occurred with the right amount of sustained energy to survive. A variation of this flight response is to freeze or hide—just like the proverbial deer in the headlights!

The conclusion today about fight or flight is that through evolution all mammals, including us as humans, have solidly developed this physiological response in order to survive. Thousands of years ago, when it was a matter of reacting to a threat, most likely a physical one, like being chased by a predator, the body responded physiologically, returned to its normal state, and did not remain in a state of stress. But how much of today's stress is physical? Currently, you could fear a terror attack if you live in a war-torn country, but on Main Street, USA, how many terror attacks occur daily? Similarly, the recent rash of school shootings is clearly a physical threat. While these are not everyday events, the fear they cause can be a great source of stress. This is a perception, or undercurrent, that could live in your subconscious and perpetuate the release of stress hormones. This is why, today, stress is often called a *lifestyle* disease. Stress is ubiquitous!

While the stress response was an asset in the Stone Age for survival, today it is literally killing us. Our bodies respond to stress physically in the same way they did in the Stone Age—that is, they produce stress hormones regardless of the cause of the stress. Physically, this results in two processes. The first set of stress hormones addresses the short-term response, causing increased heart and breathing rates, reduced activity in the stomach, reduced saliva production (dry mouth), dilated pupils, and glucose release into the bloodstream. The second process addresses the sustained stress reaction. It causes the liver to release stored glucose to maintain a ready supply of fuel for the body while it suppresses the immune system. "The activation and effects of the long-term stress response are similar to those of the short-term; however, maintaining a raised heart and breathing rate, inhibited digestion, and so on over prolonged periods of time has negative health consequences."[8] Whether the threat is physical, emotional, psychological, environmental, infectious, or some combination thereof, our bodies react! Now let's consider what the perception of these many kinds of threats might do to us.

The Physiology of Perceived Threats

Just as Cannon provided breakthrough insights on the basic physiology of the stress reaction, Hans Selye, MD, and research followers originated and supported the theory that the fight or flight response in humans has not adapted to threats to the mind, emotion, or spirit.[9] Further, his research provided links to diseases of the kidneys, heart, and blood vessels and those linked to inflammation and immune disorders such as rheumatoid arthritis as well as depression. These issues are now considered lifestyle diseases, the same diseases linked to the leading causes of death noted earlier.

In 2009, Robert M. Sapolsky built on this theory with his book *Why Zebras Don't Get Ulcers*.[10] His premise is that the human stress response is a reaction not only to physical threats, such as a bear chasing you for getting near its honey, but also to perceived mental, emotional, and spiritual threats. The problem is these threats don't subside; thus, our bodies are in a continual state of heightened physiological tension. This creates a rich environment for lifestyle disease to prevail as our bodies don't return to a resting state, or homeostasis. We can think of it as a car that is running, and when it pulls into the garage, it keeps on running and never quits, emitting dangerous toxins.

My friend Nicole who had the voicemail message from her physician's office late on that Friday afternoon was filled with fear in listening to it. On hearing the tone of voice and message, she perceived the worst. She didn't have any facts about the result of her test. She made a fear-filled assumption and perceived what she thought was to come. Her fight or flight physiological response was loud and clear, producing physical reactions in her body. There was no place to run for safety to make it subside.

Just like Nicole, when a stressful situation, a threat, is recognized in our brains, we make a decision based on what we experience in the moment and on our stored experiences and memories. Knowingly or unknowingly, emotion is evoked, and our brains automatically trigger our physiological systems to react. We know that all people react the same way physically in producing stress hormones despite the fact that we all perceive stressful events and situations differently. Another patient from Nicole's physician's office may have received the same exact message and heard it as "all is well." This person was in homeostasis and then went off to have a great weekend!

When we react as Nicole did in this situation, we are in the opposite of homeostasis. We are trying to adjust to a lifestyle of perpetual fight or flight with no place to run and no way to turn off the stress hormones. Our breathing, respiration rate, blood pressure, and absence or presence of neurotransmitters in our brain, to name a few factors, are out of balance. This can contribute to illness.

A headline in a *Huffington Post* article read "10 Weird Signs You're Stressed Out: Your Body Might Be Trying to Tell You Something."[11] The signs of stress the article details seem endless: throbbing muscles, headache, thirst, sweating, hair loss, tooth troubles, foggy memory, and more. The point is, our bodies are trying to tell us something, and we need to take action to address it. The something is not a single, physical threat. It is most likely the unconscious undercurrent of many stressors, perceived or not. Some of these stressors could be the buried emotion of trauma experienced in the near or distant past.

In today's twenty-first-century context, chronic stress prevails and the chase seems to be never ending, resulting in ongoing negative health outcomes that often prove fatal.[12] Stress has become common and is often taken for granted as just part of life. But the integrated systems in our bodies are operating in exception mode. It is not a matter of our bodies working to fight off a disease related to a bacterial infection, in which case, when given a ten-day round of antibiotic, we are usually all better! With stress, our bodies have to fight to combat our lifestyle! To better manage stress, understanding the types of stress is important. So here we go.

THE DIMENSIONS OF STRESS

Researchers have classified stress in many different ways. Pertinent to the types of stress we experience in our lives today, figure 1.1 presents the dimensions of stress. The upper portion shows the model developed by psychologist Richard Lazarus depicting the continuum of good to bad stress.[13] The lower portion shows frequency and intensity. Each is discussed below.

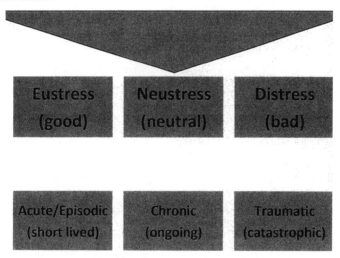

Figure 1.1.   The Dimensions of Stress

Good, Bad, or Neutral Stress

While all this talk about stress might lead you to conclude it's all bad, it's not! Midcentury research by Hans Selye was the foundation for Richard Lazarus's work, who offered three basic definitions. They are *eustress*, *neustress*, and *distress*.[14]

Eustress is good stress that is inspiring or fulfilling. It might result in a rapid heartbeat and perspiration when asking your significant other to marry and they say yes, for example. In general, good stress is short-term and pushes you to accomplish greater things. In these situations, you tend to have a lot of control over the outcome, and the stress can motivate you.

At the opposite end of the spectrum is distress. This type of stress is negative and is the general connotation of stress. Distress might cause despair, grief, and extreme sadness. An example of a stressor that can cause distress is the death of a spouse or natural catastrophe like a hurricane causing major havoc or for you to lose your home. Bad stress is often accompanied by feelings of helplessness because you don't have a lot of control over what's happening, and you may begin to feel trapped and unable to cope with a wide range of emotions. Your perception of stress is critical too. A divorce for one person could be the worst thing they have ever experienced, and for another person it could be a huge relief and time to party!

Neustress is neutral stress. It is something that produces neither a good nor a bad response in you. Recently, while having lunch with a friend, I overheard a conversation at the next table between two people discussing their auto repair woes. While it sounded like one of them had a huge mess they were dealing with, I had no reaction as it had no immediate effect on me. I was therefore neutral about the whole situation. If, however, I had experienced a recent repair that had been a major hassle in my life, hearing that conversation could have turned my neutral feelings into distress causing a physical reaction. It's all a matter of your perception.

Here's an example of how perception feeds your stress reaction in good and bad ways. Joe is an avid skier who loves being outdoors. He loves the thrill of speeding downhill, rounding the turns, and navigating the moguls. He is also very competitive with his ski buddies and puts a lot of pressure on himself to excel. The eustress he experiences is the mere anticipation of the first run of the day and motivation for a great day on the slopes. He is looking forward to the accolades he expects to receive for his speed and prowess at the end of the day.

However, as the day continues and the snow conditions deteriorate due to rising temperatures, he tires and perceives he is doing the worst in comparison to his buddies. Physically, he feels nauseous and his head aches. Emotionally, he is angry with himself. And mentally, his inner critic is attacking his ego and telling him he's a loser with a capital *L*. His self-doubt generates fear and causes him to lose focus. He questions his ability to simply get down the hill without falling. Joe's ability to recognize his distress and manage it is critical to his well-being and health. Does any of this resonate with you?

Acute and Episodic Stress

The National Institute of Mental Health defines some stress as the following:

1. *Acute stress* is brought about by a sudden change and is generally short-term by nature. An example is a new job; it could be eustress (good), distress (bad), or neustress (neutral).
2. *Episodic stress* is also short term by nature but occurs more than once. College students preparing for and taking a test might experience episodic stress. Once the exam is over, they are able to return to their normal lifestyle. While stressful in nature, the stress experienced is usually temporary, and most people recover in a short period of time.

These two types of stress are similar in that they are about the impact of big and small life events. The difference is the degree of frequency. Ruth, for example, on her way to work one day had a minor traffic accident. There was no major damage to either car. She and the driver exchanged contact information, and both agreed there was no follow-up required. It created some stress for her that day as she pondered the what-ifs of the collision. By the next day, she had put the whole incident out of her mind.

Another travel example is stress related to flying. Charlie's work requires him to fly to New York City from Washington, D.C., to meet with his boss monthly. Charlie doesn't mind flying so much, but he is extremely anxious about flying into LaGuardia Airport because there is usually lots of air traffic, along with holding pattern delays, and he feels uneasy about the approach to landing over the river. Monthly he dreads the trip and episodically *stresses out*. Once the trip is over and he is safely back home, he feels neutral about that episode until the next month. In the meantime, he has been doing this literally for years and has never had a major issue.

Understanding the difference in types of events we encounter and their impact is important as we decide how to manage our stress. Also critically important is our perception of the event, whether acute or episodic, and the tools we choose to manage it. To understand these differences and their correlation to illness from a personal viewpoint, we wanted to share this key research about the types of events, their degree of stress, and their impact on health.

Chronic Stress

The U.S. National Institutes of Health cautions that *chronic stress* is the most complex and deadly type. It is the exacerbation of stress that persists day in and day out. This could be the stress of twenty-first-century living, stemming from time management or financial concerns, or it could be the stress of being diagnosed with illness or living with a chronic disease. It is also dependent on the accumulation of worry, fear-based rumination, or perhaps repressed emotion from a past trauma.

What is known is that the human body responds physically to each type of stress in the same way even though people may experience it in different ways. For some, stress may result in headaches or irritability, and for others it may manifest itself as gastrointestinal issues or sleep-lessness. Research also shows that people living with chronic stress experience more frequent and severe viral infections, such as the flu or common cold, and measures like flu shots are less effective for them.[15]

The impact of routine stress, or perpetual rumination and worry due to a perceived threat, is said to be killing us.[16] A key factor is that it is difficult to notice the health change because the source of stress is perceived and tends to be more constant. In this way, the body gets no clear signal to return to normal functioning or, to use the biological word, homeostasis. This chronic attack on the body from routine stress has been shown to lead to serious health problems, such as, once again, heart disease, high blood pressure, diabetes, depression, anxiety disorder, and other illnesses.[17] Again, these are the leading causes of death today in the United States and in the world's higher-income countries.[18]

Traumatic Stress

Traumatic events are defined as "shocking and emotionally overwhelming situations that may involve actual or threatened death, serious injury, or threat to physical integrity."[19] As with other types of stress, there is a range of reactions to traumatic events, from minor to severely debilitating. In the world, we hear stories daily about the trauma of military conflicts, explosions, and refugees seeking asylum from conflict lands. For those of us living in the United States, a traumatic experience might be living in a community where shooting, mugging, or burglary are prevalent. Certainly, the epidemic of school shootings taking place in the United States is traumatic. Other traumatic events that are common for many Americans are physical or sexual assault/abuse in the workplace, bullying in schools, weather-related natural disasters, and being in or witnessing a serious auto accident. Whether we experience this trauma firsthand or hear about it in our daily news, these traumatic events pervade our lives.

From the history of wars in our world, there are many people who have seen brutally horrific incidents of death and carnage. Civil war veterans were said to have a "soldier's heart"; and the term *shell shocked* was often used for those who survived World War I. *Posttraumatic stress disorder* (PTSD) and *traumatic brain injury* (TBI) are all too familiar terms that emerged from more recent military engagements in countries like Iraq and Afghanistan.

The statistics about PTSD are staggering. It is reported that 7 to 8 percent of our population will experience PTSD in their lifetimes. Schoolchildren who are victims of regular bullying experience PTSD. During a given year, eight million people will have PTSD, with that being a small percentage of the individuals who have experienced a major traumatic event.

Bessel van der Kolk, MD, has dedicated his life to research and treatment of individuals who have experienced trauma. He notes that trauma may happen to any of us. One doesn't have to be a refugee from a war-torn land or a soldier who has faced gruesome combat to experience trauma. Child abuse and alcoholism are two common examples of trauma that leave a mark on the mind, body, and spirit of humans.

van der Kolk's research spanning more than three decades has profoundly shaped the current understanding of the mind–body connection. He has demonstrated the way traumatic stress affects the whole person and that our ability to gain control over the stresses of the past must address what lies deep within us. The critical conclusion he reaches is that there is no one-size-fits-all approach to helping people overcome trauma and live healthy lives.[20] Again, your perception of the threat or experience and your ability to manage your reaction are part of the solution to thriving and not surviving only, particularly with trauma.[21] His findings show there are many ways healing from trauma can occur. Insights gained from his work serve as a solid guide for learning how to manage the stress of our everyday, twenty-first-century lives.

THE STRESS AND ILLNESS CONNECTION

In the late 1960s, psychiatrists Thomas Holmes and Richard Rahe began research to evaluate the connection between life events and illness.[22] Their initial work was based on evaluation of over five thousand medical records and resulted in the publication of the Social Readjustment Rating Scale (SRRS). It is known more commonly as the Holmes and Rahe Stress Scale, and variations of it continue today as a standard to assess stress as the number of *life change units* that apply to events in the past year of an individual's life. With the Holmes and Rahe approach, the total score obtained is then used as a possible predictor of the impact of stress and illness for that individual.

Saul McLeod summarized the research of Holmes and Rahe and others who followed them.[23] In 1967, Rahe continued using the scale, and his research concluded there was a statistically significant positive correlation between experiencing stressful life events and stress-related health breakdown. In other words, as life events measured in life change units increased, so did the frequency of illness. Considering the physiology of stress, this makes logical sense given the physical changes in the body from the stress reaction and disease that occurs. While this was a useful correlation, it didn't take into consideration the way each individual might respond to an event, both reaction and perception.

Ruth in the previous example, who experienced a small auto incident, was not fearful of it occurring again. Within a day, she had pretty much forgotten that it had happened. Steve, on the other hand, while traveling on an interstate highway, once experienced cargo from an open truck, a pipe, fly through the air and shatter his windshield. He nearly lost control of the car due to the rate of speed and inability to see. Now he travels that stretch of road daily and is overcome with tension. He fears that it will occur again, perhaps causing injury or even death. The difference between these two perceptions of the stressor experienced can also be the difference between dealing with a chronic condition like hypertension or not. One person could consider this life threatening and another simply a health concern that a pill will correct.

Holmes and Rahe's chart of stressors became the foundation for another researcher's work, Allen D. Kanner, who designed the Hassles and Uplifts Scale (HSUP). The purpose of Kanner's research was to evaluate "daily hassles and uplifts" as sources of stress. The HSUP is designed to measure your attitude about daily situations. Instead of focusing on highly charged life events like the death of a spouse, marriage, or retirement, which are defined on the Holmes and Rahe Stress Scale, the HSUP provides a way to evaluate positive (uplifts) and negative (hassles) events that regularly occur in your daily life. Examples of daily hassles could be the photocopy machine jamming in the office, misplaced keys, or having an argument. Then there is the nagging hassle of looking in the mirror and seeing the ten pounds you keep trying to lose that you perceive as the reason you didn't get that long-awaited promotion. There is a whole myriad of hassles, physical and perceived. They are simply events that occur as part of the daily fabric of life. Daily uplifts, on the other hand, are simple and also part of the daily fabric of life, if you choose to look at it that way. An uplift could be having lunch with friends, a sunny day, and no traffic on the usually crowded road to work.

The HSUP consists of a list of 119 daily events designed as an assessment tool that asks you to identify which items you are currently experiencing. Next you assign a severity value of 1, somewhat severe; 2, moderately severe; or 3, extremely severe. The summation of the score provides a way to determine if you are experiencing more than average stress from the daily ups and downs of life, which puts you at greater risk for stress-related illness.[24]

The outcome of Kanner's research concluded the HSUP tended to be a more accurate predictor of stress-related issues for people than the earlier Holmes and Rahe Stress Scale because most people don't experience major, stressful, or traumatic life events, like the death of a spouse, daily. The big takeaway from these and subsequent studies is that *stress positively correlates with illness.*[25]

SOURCES OF STRESS

Personal Stressors

Just as there is a variety of types of stress, there is a huge variety of sources of stress. In 1967, the Holmes and Rahe Stress Scale listed forty-three items in order of severity, most to least, as sources of stress linked to illness. The top ten items are often noted when causes of stress are discussed. They are death of a spouse, divorce, marital separation, imprisonment, death of a close family member, personal injury or illness, marriage, dismissal from work, marital reconciliation, and retirement.

While this list was created in the mid-twentieth century, many of the items remain valid over fifty years later. It's interesting, however, to consider these stressors in the context of the era. For example, the number two item on the list is divorce. In 1967, the U.S. divorce rate was 26 percent.[26] Today, the average divorce rate is 50 percent.[27] In 1967, depending on your perspective, whether from a societal or religious view, divorce had a stigma associated with it that today is not the same, given the acceptance and frequency of divorce.

What's your reaction to these ten items? Whether recently or at some point in the last few decades, how did you react to these or similar stressors?

Our twenty-first-century living adds to these lists with stressors such as the current digital lifestyle, cell phone addiction, financial challenges, and information overload with texts, tweets, emails, videos, and social media reveals. Also, today's pace of life is much more rapid than it was in the mid-twentieth century. The stressors listed by Holmes and Rahe largely persist today. But important to consider is the pace at which change occurs with these events and the numbers of them. Additionally, noted stress researcher Richard Lazarus in 1984 hypothesized that the accumulation of small stressors like daily traffic, a bad work situation, ongoing financial woes, or daily demanding deadlines is just as impactful on one's health as Holmes and Rahe's number one stressor, the death of a spouse.[28]

Another perspective on the stressors in our current era is defined by the American Institute for Preventative Medicine.[29] Their viewpoint is that stressors are different for different people, and that they are a function of our own experience. They emphasize that adaption is required with a situation or event. Their list of seven types of stressors includes the following:

1. **Ripple Effect Stressors:** This is a series of events that are interrelated. An example is loss of employment, causing inability to pay for housing or kids' school tuition, and all the change that ensues if no comparable employment can be found.
2. **Chronic Stressors:** These are long-term stressful situations that have no resolution in sight. Being underpaid and overworked in a profession while being the sole source of finances for your family is an example.
3. **Acute Stressors:** These are short-term stressful situations that reach a resolution relatively quickly. Examples include temporary road construction causing delays for your daily commute or a home renovation.
4. **Not-Knowing Stressors:** When faced with the unknown, some of us can be highly stressed out. This could be a business trip to meet a new client for the first time in a strange city.
5. **Personal or Nonpersonal Stressors:** These stressors are caused by things that cannot be controlled. Example: being stuck due to a mechanical issue with an airplane.
6. **Trigger Stressors:** These are instances where you've experienced a stressful situation in the past and fear it will repeat. I have a fear of heights, and when approaching a large suspension bridge, the physical symptoms of stress are front and center for me.

7. **Daily Hassles:** Those minor annoyances that happen daily can add up to become a big part of your stress load. Examples: your daily commute, knowing you need to exercise but have no time to do so, or perhaps anxiety about a test or meeting with your boss.

The big question in light of these stressors is, what is your source of ongoing stress? Can you name it? What are the examples of stress in your life, and what do you do about them, or don't do?

Today's Societal Stressors

While the Holmes and Rahe studies over the past many decades considered social influence, our twenty-first-century, fast-paced living has sparked studies about current-day stress indicators. Since 2007, the American Psychological Association has completed its nationwide annual survey on stress as part of their focus on health and well-being. Its purpose is to identify attitudes and behaviors about stress, how Americans react to stress, and also how we manage it.[30]

Other leading organizations studying the link between stress and health also conduct ongoing studies, including Harvard's T. H. Chan School of Public Health and the Robert Wood Johnson Foundation. These studies have identified a number of socially influenced stressors with highlights presented below.[31]

College Stress

The transition to college involves moving from dependence on the family structure to independence filled with choices. Learning to live with roommates with perhaps diverse backgrounds, life decisions about majors, academic deadlines, loans and financial challenges, and lifestyle behaviors such as drinking, drugs, and peer group pressures are only a few examples.

Workplace Stress

Workplace stress issues are due to the following: 46 percent workload, 28 percent people issues, 20 percent juggling work/life balance, and 6 percent job security. Today's organizations feel the adverse impact of stress their employees experience with the high cost of absenteeism and quality and profitability issues.

In addition to the individual human cost it imposes, U.S. businesses incur expenses of over $30 billion a year in lost work days alone.[32] The same questions persist whether you are a stressed-out individual or organization. They are: What can we do about stress in a simple, timely way? How do we relieve ourselves of the stress we feel every day and its harmful effect on our health?

Socioeconomic and Political Stress

In the February 15, 2017, "Stress in America: Coping with Change" report, an increase of stress-related symptoms from 71 percent in August 2016 to 80 percent in January 2017 was noted. This increase is largely attributed to perceptions of the current political climate, personal safety, and police violence. To sum it up, Katherine C. Nordal, PhD, the American Psychological Association's executive director for professional practice, said, "We know that chronic stress can take a toll on a person's health. It can make existing health problems worse, and even cause disease, either because of changes in the body or bad habits people develop to cope with stress. The bottom line is that stress can lead to real physical and emotional health consequences."[33]

While stress is a challenge for us as individuals, its impact is also profound for employers and educators. The many types of stressors in our current environment abound. Today's media is filled with news of political tension, issues in polarized relationships, race and gender bias, and factors such as the impact of climate change. These are just a few more to add to the list.[34]

MANAGING STRESS

Just as there are a multitude of types of stress and stressors identified by leading sources, there are also a multitude of ways presented to manage stress. Whether you go to popular sources on the internet, governmental health sources such as the CDC or National Institutes of Health, your favorite magazine, or your healthcare provider, the suggestions abound.

Common suggestions for stress management are to avoid caffeine, exercise, get plenty of sleep, and eat a proper diet. Then there are suggestions to smile, relax, take a break from your stressor. That's a tall order if that stressor is your crying baby or persistently empty bank account. Over thirty-five years ago, Dr. Jon Kabat-Zinn introduced the practice of mindfulness-based stress reduction (MBSR). It is considered a valid tool for stress management with ongoing research regarding its efficacy.

Exercise has been shown to be an excellent way to both relieve and manage stress. There are hierarchies presented as to the best types of exercise to engage in. Commonly noted is the fact that when you exercise your body releases hormones called endorphins that are proven to counteract stress hormones. Exercise is also noted as a way to clear your mind by focusing on a positive activity, to avoid ruminating on that stressful perception that might be haunting you.[35] This is helpful in treating the symptom of the stress response. While stress management tools have been shown to valuably support reducing the symptoms of stress, we question whether these stress management tools are also effective in addressing the *cause* or source of your stress and what you choose to do about it.

THE RESEARCH IS CLEAR

There are proven links between stress and disease with harmful, sometimes fatal effects on well-being and health. Beyond a reasonable doubt, research from over the last one hundred years shows that the effect of mind over body in creating illness is real; our current stress-filled lifestyle is literally killing us. Stress management tools in current practice are useful to treat the symptoms of stress but are not enough. What is needed, clearly, is a lifestyle practice to understand the cause of our stress and then move us forward to a lifestyle that turns off the ill effects of stress—what our bodies currently cannot do on their own—and helps us to sustain healthy behaviors to optimize well-being.

Brian Seaward, MD, a leading expert on stress, emphasizes that the questions of life's meaning must be addressed to get at the heart and soul of the problem.[36]

From our personal experience and pursuit of optimal well-being in the face of stress and life-threatening illness, we have learned firsthand three key takeaways:

1. To address stress and its toll on our bodies, we must understand the causes in deeply held emotion and why it matters to us to address them.
2. To change habits and behaviors that perpetuate the causes and symptoms of stress and disease, positive action is required, again based on the understanding of what matters most.
3. To develop a new lifestyle and live it, we need the right tool(s) to support us in our journey.

In reading this list, you might be feeling stressed about personally needing to address these as to-do items. From our experience and with our clients, the good news is writing is the very tool to help you! It works especially well when combined with proven practices to support sustained behavior change to eliminate or reduce stress. In the next chapter we present the research that demonstrates the proven benefits of writing as a tool to boost health and well-being. This link between stress, health, and writing is the foundation of our integrated writing methodology Write to Be Well.

2

WRITING

Your Passport to Health and Well-Being

Stress, whether an unconscious undercurrent in your life or a rampage of emotions building to mountainous proportions, can make you sick if you don't manage it. As you learned in chapter 1, stress today is considered a lifestyle disease. Everyone experiences it differently. You may feel crushing fatigue, tension across your shoulders, a clenched jaw, upset stomach, weight gain, or ongoing insomnia. It might appear as emotional symptoms like anxiety, depression, impatience, and irritability. For others, there may be no symptoms at all, until stress manifests as a major health crisis. The list of possible responses to stress is never ending. You want to tone down the stress, but you don't know how. Write to Be Well is the place to start.

There are four types of writing that are foundational to our integrated Write to Be Well method. They are expressive, affirmative, action scripting, and reflective writing. In this chapter, you'll learn how leaders in the fields of psychology and behavior change tested their theories and concluded writing is a scientifically valid vehicle to improve mental and physical health, as well as sustain behavior change. We've incorporated their research findings into our unique integrated methodology. This approach ultimately empowers you to commit to using writing to manage your stress and make lifestyle changes to enhance your well-being.

THE BENEFITS OF WRITING

Before we get into the research, let's look at some of the benefits of writing reported by professional writers and nonwriters alike. Authors like Louise DeSalvo, who wrote *Writing as a Way of Healing*, have long claimed the healing properties of writing. DeSalvo says, "Writing has *changed* my life. Writing has *saved* my life."[1] She adds, "I use my writing as a way of fixing things, of making them better, of healing myself . . . to see where I am, where I've been and where I'm going."[2] She then quotes other authors who have similar experiences with writing.

- Alice Walker, author of *The Color Purple*, said, "[It's] a matter of necessity, and that you write to save your life is really true and so far it's been a very sturdy kind of ladder out of the pit."[3]
- Henry Miller, in a letter published in *Art and Outrage*, said, "The more I wrote, the more I became a human being. . . . I was getting the poison out of my system."[4]
- Anais Nin, essayist, novelist, and writer of short stories, said, "We write to taste life twice, in the moment and in retrospect."[5]

These authors attest to the value of writing. They affirm writing clears the mind, promotes self-understanding, and moves them toward resolution.

But what about those of us who don't call ourselves writers—we who only write to-do lists on little sticky notes? Why do we need to write? How can the dribs and drabs scratched on paper save my life? Reduce my stress? Improve my health and well-being? People from our writing groups and consulting groups share why they write:

- Jeanne, a mother of three, says, "It never ceases to amaze me how writing can be such an eye into the heart and soul. When I write, I feel the weight of the day slip through my fingers."
- Mary Kay, a grandmother dealing with complicated family dynamics of multiple generations, says, "I find writing helps me sort through my feelings and find a new perspective, one that challenges me to come to terms with what's going on in my life."
- James, who's been struggling with Lyme disease for years, says, "When I write in my journal, the pain goes away. For me, writing

is a miracle—a substitute for the little white pill the doctor prescribed for my headaches."

- Bob, a type-A personality with a high-powered job, uses writing to
dump his irritable feelings onto the page. He says, "When I clear
the tension building in my gut, I can focus on what needs to be
done. Writing helps me blow off steam, which clears the way so I
can chart my course for the day."

These men and women are not professional writers, and some don't
even like to write, yet they've discovered writing about stressful events
in their daily lives reduces their frustration, anxiety, anger, or whatever
drives their stress. Some say it's a safety valve for their complicated
lives; for others, it helps them externalize the stress so they can find
meaning in the experience. For all of them, writing about the chaos in
their lives stops their ruminating and puts into words the troubling
events eroding their health.

THE RESEARCH BEHIND WRITE TO BE WELL

The decades of research behind each of the four types of writing integrated into the Write to Be Well method confirm writing is beneficial to
your health. In the section below, you'll learn about the documented
benefits of expressive writing, affirmative writing, action scripting, and
reflective writing.

Expressive Writing Gets to the Heart of Your Stress

Hundreds of studies worldwide demonstrate that expressive writing reduces stress and has other measurable health benefits.[6] In the Write to
Be Well method, expressive writing is the first step. This is where you
give voice to your feelings about the stressful events in your life. You
write free-form without regard to conventions, like spelling, punctuation, and subject–verb agreement. The most important part of this type
of writing is to get whatever *it* is down on paper. The words you choose
to describe your stress make the experience real and begin the process
of helping you understand a stressful, emotionally charged event.

In the mid-1980s, social psychologist James W. Pennebaker was the first to show the connection between writing, stress, and health.[7] His research and that of his colleagues over the past thirty-five years continues to provide solid evidence that writing is healing. Pennebaker took the concept from talk therapy that withholding secrets heightens stress, while confronting them is liberating and results in long-term health benefits. He questioned whether writing, rather than talking, about secrets might be equally beneficial, but with an additional advantage of being private and nonjudgmental.[8]

Prior to Pennebaker's research about disclosure through writing was the work of Austrian physician Sigmund Freud. In the late 1800s and early 1900s he and his colleagues revealed the value of disclosure through psychoanalysis, a form of psychotherapy. They proved that talking about a trauma is a natural and healthy human response to what worries you. However, when feelings of shame, inhibition, or discomfort stop you from disclosing your pain, heightened stress and illness may follow. Freud and his contemporaries believed holding back emotions was stressful, whereas emotional disclosure and sharing the details and emotional impact of difficult events meant individuals gained understanding and insight into what happened to them.[9] Pennebaker took this concept further with his studies using writing for disclosure.

Early in his research, Pennebaker asked groups of college students to write about a significant stress or trauma they had experienced. Four groups of students were asked to write for fifteen to twenty minutes in his laboratory setting for four consecutive days:

1. Group 1 was told to vent their emotions.
2. Group 2 wrote only the facts of their trauma.
3. Group 3 was to connect the facts with their emotions.
4. A control group wrote about a trivial subject such as what they were wearing.

All groups wrote only for themselves. No one else read or edited their journal entries. In postintervention follow-up, Pennebaker discovered the people who wrote about their deepest thoughts and feelings around a trauma had the greatest gains in their health. These were the people in Group 3, who connected facts with emotions. He called this form of writing *expressive writing*. The more details and emotions revealed in the writing, the better the healing response. Although some students in the expressive writing test group said they experienced sadness immediately after writing their stories, they reported improved moods, more positive outlook, greater physical health, and fewer visits to the student health center for illness within four months of writing.[10]

According to recent studies in brain science, secrets, whether driven by shame, embarrassment, or resistance to share something personal with another person, create conflict in the brain and cause the brain to release stress hormones. If there is no emotional release of the stress, the excess hormones weaken the immune system, increase blood pressure, heighten anxiety, and create a host of other ailments.[11] The multitude of research by Pennebaker and colleagues demonstrates time and again that inhibition or repressing details, thoughts, and feelings about an event is hard work and "can place people at risk for major and minor diseases."[12] Written confession, which is similar to talk therapy, reduces stress and improves health and well-being.

In my counseling practice, I have found this to be true. The clients who self-disclose their traumas and feelings make the most progress in terms of emotional healing and understanding. The time it takes them to divulge a secret varies depending on the depth and intensity of the shame associated with the event. The deeper the wound, the longer it takes to reveal the truth. Sheila, a forty-five-year-old woman who was raped when she was eight by her favorite uncle, still questions whether it was her fault. While she wanted to talk about this event, it was difficult due to the shame and embarrassment she felt. Her uncle had threatened her to tell no one. Even years later, she continued to fear what he might do if she revealed what had happened. She suffered the repercussions of fear and anxiety, sure signs of stress.

When she came to me, Sheila was unhappy and said she could no longer bury her feelings or her shame. I started our sessions by asking her to write about the incident in her journal and then allow me to read her entry silently to myself. As she learned to trust me with her story, she started sharing more openly. Her *confession*, both in writing and orally, relieved her anxiety and helped her understand that as a child she was not culpable. Sheila experienced emotional relief when she began writing and telling her story. We've all been resistant at times to share an embarrassing or shameful moment yet yearned to heed the sage advice to "just get it off your chest, you'll feel better!" When Sheila finally did, it changed her life.

Expressive writing research is based on the writing model developed by Pennebaker. In every case, the experimental group wrote about a highly stressful event and linked it to their emotions. The control group wrote about a daily event without an emotional charge, like a diary entry listing what you did on a given day. Both groups wrote for three consecutive days for twenty minutes each time. Pennebaker's and his colleagues' research over the course of more than thirty years demonstrates that writing heals not just the emotions but also the body. Here's a sampling of what's been learned from the pioneers in expressive writing research:

- **Writing boosts immune functioning.** The research team collected blood samples to gauge immune function before and after writing. They found evidence that people who wrote about their deepest thoughts and feelings about a stressful, traumatic event had heightened T-lymphocytes in their blood, the immune cells that help protect the body from abnormalities and infection.[13]
- **Writing decreases severity of asthma and rheumatoid arthritis.** In another groundbreaking study, researchers selected patients with chronic asthma or rheumatoid arthritis to determine if writing about a stressful event would have clinically relevant changes in health status. Results showed asthma patients in the experimental group showed improvements in lung function beyond those attributed to medical care, whereas the control group showed no change. Rheumatoid arthritis patients showed improvements in overall disease activity, including levels of pain, tenderness, and swelling throughout the affected joints.[14]
- **Writing improves after-care outcomes of heart attack patients.** A study assessed the effect of expressive writing on people who had recently had a heart attack, also known as a myocardial infarction. Five months postintervention, the writing group had fewer medical appointments and were taking fewer prescription medications than the control group. They were also more compliant with their after-care, having attended more rehabilitation sessions than the control group. The expressive writing group also

reported fewer cardiac-related symptoms and had lower diastolic blood pressure five months after the writing experiment.[15]

- **Writing promotes wound healing.** One study asked healthy adults, ages sixty-four to ninety-seven, to write for three consecutive days about the most traumatic experience in their lives. Two weeks after the first writing, researchers performed a small skin biopsy. Wounds were photographed every three to five days until they healed. Eleven days after the biopsy, 76 percent of the adults in the experimental group had fully healed compared with 42 percent of those in the control group.[16]
- **Writing reduces pain in patients with cancer.** Before writing, advanced cancer patients rated their pain intensity as 5 on a 0–10 scale. After writing, the findings indicated those whose expressive writing had high emotional disclosure had significantly lower pain intensity and higher well-being scores than patients whose narratives were less emotional. Although the study was a small sampling of cancer patients, the 2.5-unit decrease in pain intensity is considered by patients to be clinically meaningful.[17]

The studies based on Pennebaker's expressive writing model provide scientific evidence to prove expressive writing offers biological benefits to people battling acute and chronic disease. Along with the proof comes some cautionary notes about what expressive writing can and cannot do. "Expressive writing does not kill cancer cells or viruses associated with serious illness such as AIDS."[18] Researchers clearly state, "If you are deeply struggling to deal with a trauma or an illness, writing should not be used as a substitute or replacement for other psychological or medical treatment."[19] However, there is significant evidence from research over the past thirty-five years that expressive writing can boost immune function by reducing the cumulative effects of stress. The findings confirm, "Writing may help enhance emotional, psychological, behavioral, and biological processes that, in turn, may contribute to improvements in health and well-being."[20]

Affirmative Writing Builds Confidence in the Future

Affirmative writing is the vehicle that supports us in connecting our current reality to our desired future. The desired future may be an event, a goal, a feeling, a situation, or something else that you have articulated in your writing. With affirmative writing, we assert what we need and/or want as if it's in the present. This includes how we feel and most importantly links us to what matters, our values.

Affirmations therefore support behavior change by pronouncing a future-oriented goal to be true and by challenging our belief system that may have negative messages we tell ourselves. If you've ever dieted or tried to stop smoking, you probably have a sense of how hard it is to break old ways of doing things. That's because our belief system is stored in our subconscious mind. If you believe "I do not deserve to be fit and thin" or "I'm addicted to smoking," then it may be difficult to lose weight or stop smoking. We go through life according to our beliefs. However, we can change our behavior if we change our beliefs. That's where affirmative writing helps.

Affirmative writing demands the use of positive words to affirm rather than negate our desired future. To position yourself for a positive outcome, with the use of positive words, affirmations reframe any negative beliefs into positive ones like, "Within five years, I am thriving in my preferred job." By telling yourself this repeatedly and consciously, it becomes part of your belief system.

The words we choose to describe our beliefs and our experiences contribute to our healing capacity. This was proven with the Linguistic Inquiry and Word Count (LIWC), a computer program developed by expressive writing's Pennebaker and one of his graduate students. They analyzed the language used in a number of expressive writing studies. LIWC linked three linguistic factors to improved health: (1) the higher use of positive words, like *happy, joy, love, laughter*; (2) a moderate number of negative words, like *hate, anger, mean, nasty*; and (3) an increasing use of cognitive words, like *understand, realize, know*. The use of cognitive words was interpreted to mean people were putting a narrative together to understand their experience. Words, both those we choose to describe ourselves and those others assign to us, have the power to either uplift or discourage.[21]

Take the case of a client, Manuel, a physician who is often mistaken for someone in the service industry—maître d', parking valet, custodian—even though he's wearing a white lab coat with the name of the hospital monogrammed on the pocket. Each time this happens, he gets upset, although he usually smiles and responds pleasantly to the individual who made the error. Underneath the smile, he feels angry. Manuel doesn't feel he can talk to anyone about these confrontations. He is afraid it would sound petty. As a result, his stress escalates.

Manuel needed to get this off his chest by disclosing his feelings and shifting his perspective to focus on what is right in his life. Manuel wrote about his stress and his desired future story. He penned this affirmation: "I am a doctor who relates well to my patients and colleagues; in all contacts with them, I make a positive difference in their lives as well as in mine."

His affirmation helped him focus on what was going well in his life so that he was less defensive and irritated by negative comments. By refocusing on the positive, the comments from people he didn't know became minor blips in an otherwise fulfilling day. The affirmation shifted Manuel's perspective and alleviated the stress he experienced.

To overcome stressful messages, social psychologist Claude Steele, founder of self-affirmation theory, suggests that people like Manuel need to be reminded they are fundamentally competent, good, stable, capable of free choice, and able to control outcomes. He says, when circumstances threaten the validity of your core values, you are more likely to experience heightened stress and react defensively. Steele hypothesized that people can be affirmed either by engaging in activities that remind them of who they are or by reflecting on a personally relevant value. He believed self-affirmation would reduce the perceived threat and allow the person to act less defensively and more effectively.[22]

Jason, a participant in one of our Write to Be Well test groups, illustrates the positive effect of affirmation. Jason, a successful businessman in a high-stress sales job, travels frequently and finds it difficult to maintain an exercise program or eat three balanced meals a day. He is overweight but not obese. On a recent weekend when he was mowing the lawn, he experienced chest pains and was rushed to the hospital by ambulance. The doctor's diagnosis was acute myocardial infarction, commonly referred to as a heart attack. A coronary stent was surgically implanted to keep the artery open and improve blood flow. On release from the hospital, Jason was given information about stress management, diet, and exercise. He read the handouts but dismissed the advice, thinking it would be impossible to implement all these lifestyle changes and still work a demanding full-time job.

The new health information threatened Jason's sense of who he is—a competent man, capable of handling his job, family responsibilities, finances, and volunteer work. But Jason's health is in crisis. He's received information designed to help him live a healthy lifestyle and rejected it. His stress is running at an all-time high, and he feels like he's out of control. According to Steele's self-affirmation theory, Jason is a perfect candidate to benefit from an affirmation. He is defensive and unwilling to take the health advice seriously. Self-affirmation theory suggests Jason can reduce his resistance to the healthy lifestyle recommendations by affirming a value that is personally relevant. Jason values his involvement in humanitarian work. He is active in supporting a nonprofit organization that teaches computer skills to low-income individuals. He affirms himself by writing: "I make healthy choices to reduce my stress, eat a nutritious balanced diet, and exercise so that I will have the vitality I need for the volunteer work I care about." Jason's affirmation challenges his negative thinking by reminding him he is a competent human being with self-worth. His affirmation buffers against the stress he is experiencing by focusing his attention on something he values. Jason is more willing now to listen to the important information meant to improve and extend his life.

Steele's self-affirmation theory has been tested over the years in a variety of health settings to verify that affirmation reduces resistance to unwelcome health-risk information and improves the physiological response to stress.[23] Patients often struggle to actively engage in managing their disease, even though they know not following recommendations will jeopardize their health. It's easier to ignore beneficial health information than it is to build healthy habits into your life. It's hard to change your diet when you love fast food, or participate in physical activity when you abhor exercise, or even to adhere to a rigid medication schedule. The medical profession has turned to behavioral science theories, such as positive affect and self-affirmation, to help patients successfully change their behaviors to be in line with best health practices.

Here's a sampling of the studies from pioneers in the field of self-affirmation theory:

- In a study with type 2 diabetes patients, researchers measured participants' risk levels and examined whether affirmation would improve acceptance of threatening type 2 diabetes information. At the outset of the experiment, participants were asked to affirm a value that was either personally important or unimportant to them. The study measured the perceived value to participants of the new diabetes information and assessed their intentions to take an online type 2 diabetes risk test. The study concluded that for an at-risk population (people not inclined to follow doctor's orders), self-affirmation can decrease defensive responses to threatening health information and promote test taking for risk of diseases.[24]

- In another study to determine if self-affirmation increases health-promoting behavior, ninety-three women were randomly assigned to a self-affirmation or control group prior to reading a message about the health effects of fruit and vegetables. Both groups kept a food diary to chart fruit and vegetable consumption over the course of seven days. The findings showed self-affirmed participants ate approximately 5.5 more portions of fruit and vegetables, across the week, in comparison to the control group. The study concluded self-affirmation interventions can successfully influence health-promoting behaviors.[25]

- A key research study that evaluated the efficacy of self-affirmation concluded, "Positive affirmations can help when they are part of a broader program of intervention."[26]

Write to Be Well provides the platform for using self-affirmation theory as an integral part of your plan to promote health and well-being.

Action Scripting Challenges You to Act on Reducing Stress

Action scripting is the two-part writing process we've created to motivate you to act on your desire to reduce your stress. Up to this point, expressive writing helped you get to the core of your stress, and affirmative writing helped you name your desired future state of well-being. With action scripting you move your narrative forward by (1) writing a plan of action and (2) defining your SMART goals (specific, measurable, achievable, realistic, time bound). Action scripting is based on goal-setting theory and the way our brains process information to support behavior change.

The words associated with action scripting energize, motivate, and direct your performance. SMART goals need power verbs like *strengthen, improve,* and *accomplish.* "Marshall McLuhan, communication theorist of the 20th century, quipped that 'All words are verbs.' A single word is a source of movement and action."[27] Use strong action verbs when you script your plan and set your goals.

Goal-setting theories came about in the mid-twentieth century with studies at Yale and Harvard and research by Locke and Latham.[28] This research involved extensive laboratory and field studies that clearly indicated that participants who had specific challenging goals consistently outperformed those with vague, less challenging goals. Their studies proved the following:

- Goals energize performance.
- Goals motivate people to persist in activities through time.
- Goals direct people's attention to what is relevant to the task and away from activities not related to the goal.[29]

Locke and Latham's body of work is the foundation of today's goal setting in education, business, health, and other organizational settings. It is a proven way of motivating people and of motivating one's self.

Locke and Latham's research confirms the usefulness of SMART goal setting, and their theory continues to influence the way we measure performance today. The key conclusion that holds true over more than five decades since Locke and Latham's original studies is that individuals who set clear goals that are specific, measurable, achievable, realistic, and time bound are highly motivated to reach their goal—which in turn improves overall performance. The principles of SMART goal setting provide the mechanism and self-feedback for achieving success.

Science also proves that goal setting is even more effective when it's in the written form of a plan. From research conducted in the Harvard MBA Program in 2015, impressive results prove the point that having goals and a written plan to achieve them yields measurable results. The Harvard study explored the hypothesis of whether writing down your goals really helps or is just a myth. Harvard's graduate students were asked if they have set clear, written goals for their futures, as well as if they have made specific plans to transform their fantasies into realities.

The result of the study was that only 3 percent of the students had written goals and plans to accomplish them, 13 percent had goals in their minds but had not written them anywhere, and 84 percent had no goals at all. Think for a moment which group you belong to. After ten years, the same group of students were interviewed again, and the conclusion of the study was totally astonishing. The 13 percent of the class who had goals but did not write them down earned twice the amount of the 84 percent who had no goals. The 3 percent who had written goals were earning, on average, ten times as much as the other 97 percent of the class combined. People who don't write down their goals tend to fail more easily than the ones who have plans. This study proves that statement, even if the only criterion was the monetary reward of each Harvard graduate. When you don't have a plan with clear goals, you don't know how you will reach your destination.[30]

Studies like the Harvard one abound. Henriette Klauser, in her book *Write It Down, Make It Happen*, contributes to the case that having goals and plans makes a difference.[31] She further makes the point that the act of writing down your goals and plans makes *all* the difference. She explains that at the base of the brain is a set of cells that help us sort and evaluate incoming data. This is called the reticular activating system (RAS) and is a control center that supports us by filtering incoming information. It filters by sending the urgent "stuff" it receives to our active brain area and the nonurgent to our subconscious. The act of writing has been proven to set up a filter in the RAS that flags information as urgent. The urgent filter about what you have written provides clarity within the chaos of all the information we are bombarded with daily, stressfully. Writing down a self-affirmation reinforces our self-integrity and reminds us what we want to achieve in reducing stress and boosting health. Then, a second filter in the RAS is set when we write down our plan to make it happen. The reinforcing messages and actions needed to reduce stress and boost health are alive and active through the simple act of writing it down.

Larry, a client from our consulting days, worked in a large law firm in Washington, D.C., where it is said eight out of every ten people on the street are lawyers. He had paid his dues, worked the many hours to be billable, but never liked what he was doing nor felt he received the recognition he deserved. So he worked even harder and longer. He was stressed. Eating became his solace. He gained over fifty pounds in a year, developed high blood pressure, and his joints were swollen and painful when he walked. He felt he was a victim of the law firm's politics. His physician said something must change as his hypertension was uncontrollable.

By using action scripting, Larry took control of his own destiny. He examined his situation and how he had been viewing it. When he worked with his values and what mattered most in his life, he began to understand he did not need to be a victim of office politics. He came up with a plan for managing his stress and wrote SMART goals that reflected how he wanted to live his life. He made a commitment to change, which resulted in his improved health and a more satisfying role in his current law firm.

Action scripting integrates the principles of planning with SMART goals and harnesses the power of the brain and writing. It is a critical step in the Write to Be Well method because this is where you turn the change you desire, as reflected in your self-affirmation, into a tangible plan to make it happen. Research confirms that plans and goal setting are essential for long-lasting behavior change.

Reflective Writing Promotes Insight

Reflective writing challenges us to review life experiences by noticing how we have changed, developed, or grown from these events. The language associated with reflective writing reveals a shift in understanding of your story, your causes of stress, and why you're tolerating this tension-producing experience. "Causal" words, such as *cause, effect, reason*, and "insight" words, like *understand, realize, know*, denote a search to find meaning in personal stress or trauma.[32] With reflective writing, there is an evolution of insights from the first writing about a stress to the final narrative. Typically, more causal and insight words appear in each new rewriting of the story. The resulting shift toward resolution and understanding of the stress correlates with improvements in physical health.

"Writing comprises one of the most widely-used and effective forms of reflection that exists."[33] Reflective journal writing is proven to have a strong connection to support learning.[34] It is used in education, medicine, nursing, counseling, coaching, and professional development.

When you write, you externalize your thoughts and feelings by finding the words to adequately describe them. Then, as you continue to reflect and write, you have the opportunity to examine and question the true meaning of your feelings from a more rational perspective. With reflective writing, you can gain a deeper understanding of yourself by questioning why change needs to take place, your doubts and concerns, your level of commitment, your beliefs about yourself to achieve your goals, and the benefits you will receive. From our experience in the coaching and counseling fields, the insight gained from reflective writing is key to reducing stress and achieving optimal health and well-being.

Jaimie, one of my counseling clients who is now thirty-five years old, writes in his journal when his heart starts to race. He knows the feeling is panic, triggered by an old memory. He lost his mother in a car accident when he was just four. He was a passenger in the backseat. All he remembers from that day are the screaming, the silence, and then the sirens. He was intensely frightened and became mute for weeks. He had no words for what happened to him. By working with a child psychologist, he was finally able to reenact the scene with the help of play therapy. Although his language skills were limited by his four-year-old vocabulary, he eventually told the therapist in simple words what happened. Years later, Jaimie admits there are times when he is still traumatized by a siren. Now he knows he can break the panic cycle by writing about it. Although he's written the story many times, when he reflects on the experience, he goes deeper into his emotions, the meaning of the experience, and its impact on his life. The writing helps him detach from the trauma and accept that he had no role in this tragedy. He says, "I no longer feel victimized by this event. When I write, I can be a witness without judgment." Over the years, Jaimie's perspective has shifted, and with each rewriting of his story, the grip of the trauma loses a little more of its hold on his life.

Research demonstrates that writing helps us organize and integrate the troubling stories that haunt us and identify the emotions that fuel stress and undermine health. Reflecting on and writing about emotional events releases pent-up stress and gives people a new perspective on the event. The problems that seemed insurmountable before may be more manageable after seeing them on paper. With the act of writing, there is no longer a need to ruminate over the problem; when your understanding increases, your stress levels go down.[35]

To put it another way, when your world gets turned upside down, you need to find meaning in the experience—the silver lining, if there is one. If you can do that through writing, you begin to see some of the good that comes out of that experience. Reflective writing has the potential to help you make sense of your world, to look for benefits in the experience, and to boost your sense of self-efficacy, which when applied to your health means you become an instrument of your own change.

Wayne Dyer, author and motivational speaker, is frequently quoted as saying, "If you change the way you look at things, the things you look at change."[36] Reflective writing is a way to change the way you review the outcome of your expressive writing, self-affirmation, and action scripting. By reflecting on all your writing, you decide if what you've stated still rings true for you. Are you really ready to *change* the way you look at your life? If you are, are you ready to commit to the change you want to achieve? As Shaun McNiff, a leading scholar on the expressive arts, says, "Words become agents of transformation . . . and transport people to change."[37] They help us to see the compelling reason why we need to commit to action and sustain it.

Reflective writing is the vehicle through which you consider what you have learned about yourself in your previous writings. This is where growth takes place and the commitment to a life of health and well-being becomes a reality.

TO SUM UP . . .

Writing is a powerful tool you can use to reduce your stress and optimize your health. It's an ancient craft, now reconfigured as a four-step method to help identify what's stressing you and what action you can take to make it better. Consider these proven benefits:

- **Writing is effective** because it is a form of disclosure, words are powerful, and with your words, you can find meaning in your experiences.
- **Expressive writing** provides the foundation for identifying the emotions associated with stress and trauma, the frustrations and

heartaches of life, and the challenges of living with acute or chronic disease.

- **Affirmations** express the vision of a future with well-managed stress and optimal health. Research verifies that affirmative writing boosts self-esteem and buffers against stress and trauma.
- **Action scripting** provides the platform for designing a step-by-step action plan with SMART goals to achieve a future life with reduced stress.
- Finally, **reflective writing** supports learning and can serve as a catalyst for change.

In the next section, you'll see how these four writing types are integrated into one dynamic writing method designed to help you manage your stress. We introduce you to the four key steps and their corresponding writing prompts; then, you'll meet Paul, a heart attack victim, and see how he used Write to Be Well as his passport back to health. We invite you to use your pen or keyboard and learn how you can write away the mountain of stress that saps your energy and chips away at your health and vitality.

Section 2

Write to Be Well

Four Easy Steps

We've always been action oriented. It was common for us to meet for a run before our respective days began. Running was one of the tools in addition to yoga and journaling that we used to manage the daily stress of juggling kids' activities, schedules, work, and the simple ups, downs, and issues of life.

To this day, we both have a lasting memory of one of those runs and conversations about our journaling. We honestly don't remember who started the conversation, but we *do* remember the lasting impression it made that we both found ourselves writing about the same issues over and over rather than being proactive and doing something about it. Being honest with ourselves, we declared it was whining, not doing, and recognized we were stuck in our old stories. We needed something more to live true to our value of being action oriented and doing more than managing an issue versus eliminating or minimizing it.

Over the years, we each took different classes and engaged in a variety of programs and activities seeking the right path for optimizing health, well-being, and the ability to manage time and life rather than being a victim of it. There were graduate school programs and individual classes about affirmations, positivity, gratitude, self-actualization, psychology, counseling, coaching, and more. We were each relentless in digging deeply to understand the whys and wherefores about each subject area and not simply doing it as a matter of rote exercise.

A few years ago, with this depth of learning, combined with our life and professional experience, our *aha* was that individually these things were *great*, and they were even *greater* when integrated into this writing method, which we found had not been done before. The method worked, and still works for us and for the others we've shared and tested it with. Now we need and want to share it with you. Goodness knows that our stress-ridden world and lives need simple, effective, affordable tools so we can not only survive but thrive. What you will find here is an integrated four-step method of writing to support you in living with less stress and optimal health. That's why we call it Write to Be Well!

Simply said, the first three steps of the method are about telling your story, identifying what's bugging you, what you value, what you want and need to change, and creating a realistic plan of action to do something about it; whatever *it*, your stress, is. The fourth step is reflectively writing to commit yourself to achieving your goals and making it happen. We've heard from more than one of the users of this method that Write to Be Well is like a self-coach that supports them on their life's journey every day. Figure 2.1 presents graphically the four integrated steps.

KEY ELEMENTS OF WRITE TO BE WELL

The method is designed as a flexible and scalable tool to be used whether you are an experienced writer, a person who has journaled over the years, or someone who has never written or perhaps has a fear of writing. In our writing workshops and test groups, the spectrum of writing experience is from none to a lifetime of writing.

The emphasis with Write to Be Well is not on composition, style, grammar, punctuation, or spelling. The emphasis is on expressing and connecting your thoughts, feelings, emotions, and actions to support the change you need and want to make. Your writing is for your eyes only, unless you choose to share it. You can write with paper and pen or pencil or you can write with a word processor. We do encourage you to do at least some of your writing by hand for your action items, based on

Write To Be Well Method

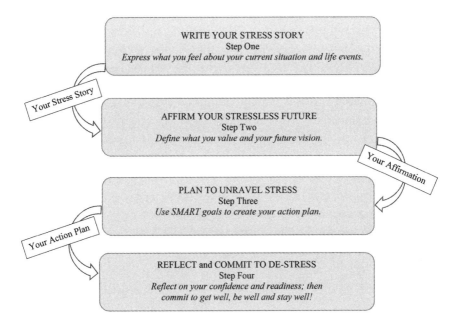

Figure 2.1. The Integrated Steps of Write to Be Well

the research presented in chapter 2 that the physical act of writing something down gives it a lasting place in your brain.

Important to note is that this integrated method is not a substitute for professional medical, psychological, or emotional help. It is designed, however, and proven to be useful by both individuals and professionals in the healing arts and coaching professions. Whether you are a practitioner helping a patient or client or a novice or experienced writer using this methodology, it can be used on your own or in the context of a larger treatment plan. Why? Because Write to Be Well provides a new tool and path to support stress management, behavior change, and healing. Its use leads to better physical, mental, and emotional health.

HOW TO USE THIS SECTION

In this section, you will find four chapters, each dedicated to one of the four steps in Write to Be Well. Each chapter provides instruction and helpful tips. At the end of chapter 6, you will find a summary of the four steps with their writing prompts for your future use.

Within each chapter, there is a demonstration of the step using the actual journal entries of Paul, who granted us use of his story. His name has been changed to preserve his privacy. As Paul's story unfolds in each chapter, you will learn he had a massive heart attack and needed to reduce stress and establish a healthy lifestyle. This is easy to say but not necessarily easy to do. You will see with his example a basic way Write to Be Well can be used as a stress management tool.

For each step, you can expect to learn the following:

- How to execute the step using writing prompts,
- The unique characteristics of the writing you will do,
- The process of reflection to guide you in your next action,
- The recommended frequency and duration of writing for the prompts.

As you will see, the steps build on one another in the context of the integrated methodology. The first time you write using the method, it is important to complete each step sequentially, so you can learn and experience how they interrelate. Ultimately, you will find that each step is a powerful tool that can be used anytime, anywhere, for as long or short as you wish and find meaningful.

Once you have experienced all four steps, you may find that you choose to use the steps in a different combination or ways. Later, in Sections 3 and 4, we share stories and helpful tips on using Write to Be Well to deal with both large and small issues in your life.

WRITING GUIDELINE SUMMARY

Here's a quick summary of the general writing guidelines for use as reference with each step. In each chapter, you will find additional guidelines specific to that step.

1. **Commit to writing on a regular basis,** but on your own time schedule. You may choose to write in response to each of the writing prompts in one "sitting" or space it out throughout the day or week. Fit the writing into your schedule, for your convenience.

2. **Reflect on your writing.** We suggest that you give yourself a little time between each prompt to reflect on what you've written. This is a helpful practice to develop. We call it "Notes to Self" that you can think of as feedback on your writing.

3. **Simply write! Just dump the words onto the paper or computer.** With each prompt, write continuously. Set the timer for the recommended time for each prompt! Setting the timer is a proven practice that yields the benefit of not allowing that small voice in your head to stop you in your tracks and cast doubt or criticism on what you've written. Longer is okay as long as it is not an exercise in composition, analysis, or perfection.

4. **Write for your eyes only.** Do not be concerned about grammar, punctuation, or style as the writing is for your benefit. Anything you write is for your eyes only, unless you choose to share it with another. We suggest you have a special place to secure your journal if that level of privacy is important to you.

5. **Be honest with yourself!** Allow yourself to be completely authentic and truthful with yourself. This can sometimes be difficult, and at the same time the reward will be great to state those thoughts, words, or feelings that are not acknowledged yet impacting you and your health. Remember, you are writing for yourself and your well-being.

6. **Techniques!** If you are a first-time writer, get ready to learn different writing techniques with each of the prompts.

While the writing guidelines are proven to help you get the most out of your writing, there is no absolutely right or wrong way to do it. Your story is your narrative. Your future story is yours to create. Let's begin!

3

YOUR STORY

Tell It!

What's really bugging you? It may be a big, hairy, audacious problem, a collection of things that is an undercurrent of stress for you, or it might simply be something small that just keeps bugging you. Whatever it is, the best way to begin this writing journey is to write your thoughts and feelings about the tension that's brought you to this point.

Step One is based on the expressive writing we shared the roots, research, and evolution of in chapter 2. It's an important first step because Step One: Write Your Stress Story is the anchor for the steps and prompts that follow in the Write to Be Well method.

As a quick recap, expressive writing encompasses writing about your experiences that may be past, present, or future, real or imagined. It is a mode of writing that helps you to connect thoughts and feelings, ideas and actions, hopes and dreams, perhaps the rational and intuitive thoughts, to the details of your life experience. Research verifies the life-changing results that are possible with this writing.

Within this step, your writing will help you identify the emotions associated with your stress, the frustrations and heartaches of life, and the challenges of living that will define the current state you are in. It is essential for you to name the emotions you are experiencing so they don't fester, causing disease somewhere in your mind or body. For this reason, it is important to do more than merely vent your emotions or keep writing the same thing over and over. Some people may get stuck in their journal writing. Instead, delve deeply and name the details while also considering the why behind the stress that brings up your emotions. Your challenge is to uncover new awareness. This could be how the suffering has affected you, what you value and hope for in the future, or maybe a shift in attitude. Now on to the basics of Step One.

GUIDELINES FOR STEP ONE

Purpose: The purpose of this step is to write the story that matters most to you right now by expressing your thoughts, feelings, and emotions and then connecting them to the details of your experience.

- **Contents:** This step has three writing prompts and a reflective writing exercise.
- **Duration:** It's best to limit yourself to writing for fifteen to twenty minutes per prompt session. Literally, set the timer because knowing you have a prescribed time limit helps you focus, get started, and get to the point. This will help you to simply write your story, wherever you begin, to allow the details and emotions to arise. If at the end of the twenty minutes you need to keep writing, go ahead and let it flow. If you are feeling particularly overwhelmed with thoughts and emotions, this disclosure technique of simply writing down your emotions is useful to relieve stress.
- **Frequency:** It is your choice if you wish to complete all three prompts in one writing session or write over a period of days. You may find value in spacing out the days you write to have time for reflection between your writing sessions. This is strictly your choice and according to your schedule.
- **Reminders:** The reflection exercise is an opportunity to give yourself feedback on what you have expressed. If you feel the need, go back and restate what you've written to gain more clarity. The "Writing Guideline Summary" in the Section 2 introduction provides the general principles that are useful with all four Write to Be Well steps.

STEP ONE: WRITE YOUR STRESS STORY

Below are the basic instructions for Step One. By following the prompts and guidelines in these instructions, you will learn the core writing activities in the Write to Be Well method for this step. In Sections 3 and 4 you will find helpful tips on using Write to Be Well in other scalable and flexible ways once you master these basics. By scalable, we mean you can apply the method to either large or small issues you're facing. By flexible, we mean, once you learn the method, you can pick and choose the prompts that serve you best in the moment.

Immediately following the Step One exercises, you will find the first segment of the ongoing example of Paul's use of Write to Be Well. It begins with a summary of Paul's background and situation followed by his actual Step One responses. Again, Paul is a fictitious name for a person who granted us permission to use his story and journal entries. Now it's your turn to begin writing!

Prompt One: Complete This Sentence Stem

> The stressful situation (real or perceived) I am facing is . . .

Sentence stems are essentially a launching pad for you to get started. The sentence stem begins the thought, and you simply finish the sentence by expressing the ending and then continuing to write whatever else you want to say until you're finished with it. Go for it!

Prompt Two: Write Your Own Story

> Write your story from the "I" perspective (first person), describing your thoughts and feelings surrounding the stressful situation, real or perceived.

Explore your very deepest emotions that arise from and about the situation you've identified in your Prompt One response. Include as many details as you can and dive deeply into how you feel or felt. Consider the links between your story and the emotions you've named. As you explore this stress, you might write about its associations with other parts of your life, such as your childhood, relationships, or experiences that are important to you. You may need or want to write your story more than once. Write it as many times as you feel you need and reflect on what you have written to be sure you are continuing to uncover new things.

Prompt Three: Shift Your Perspective

Now write your story from another person's point of view (third person).

Consider what that person might observe about you. This third person could be a coworker, a family member, a stranger, a physician; it is someone you feel can provide an observation of you from a different viewpoint. Write his or her observation of how they see stress shaping or influencing your life and perhaps the situation and emotions they see you experiencing. Consider the issues about which they might think you are most vulnerable. In the same way as in Prompt One, let the words flow to express yourself from this third person's viewpoint.

Notes to Self: Reflection

Once you've finished writing, wait fifteen to thirty minutes and then reread what you've written. This can be an amazing experience. We call it "Notes to Self." Reflect on the thoughts, events, issues, and feelings that you've disclosed. Then, we encourage you to just start writing.

Remember, this writing is for your eyes only. You don't have to plan what you write. It's an opportunity to tell yourself what you think by answering these five questions. Respond to the questions that you feel are most appropriate, and allow how you feel in the moment to direct you.

1. What did you learn about yourself in responding to the prompts?
2. What did you notice about how stress plays out in your life? Did anything surprise you? Disappoint you? Annoy you? If so, be sure to name it!
3. What emotions did you uncover?
4. What happened in your body as you wrote? Did you experience any release of stress, or did you experience heightened anxiety?

5. Do you have clarity about the source of your stress, your thoughts, your feelings, and what they are "doing" to you? If not, you may want to go back and repeat the prompts.

STEP ONE KEY ELEMENTS

This step, being the first, sets the foundation for those that follow. To gain mastery with expressive writing, it is important to execute these practices:

- Write as many details as you can remember about the event, incident, or what happened, real or perceived.
- Express your emotions freely, remembering that this writing is for your eyes only unless you invite someone else to read it.
- Link the details of the situation or event to your emotions. For example, in the story you will read about Paul, he states he had a heart attack and acknowledges in his writing how scared he was.
- Express what is meaningful for you. There are multiple ways meaning can be expressed. It could be finding the silver lining in a negative experience, it could be gaining a new awareness or attitude, or perhaps it's disclosing in your writing something you have never shared with another person.
- Name or articulate what is really bugging you! Is it that something major, something minor, or a collection of things create that unconscious undercurrent of stress that is today's lifestyle disease?

PAUL'S STEP ONE JOURNEY WITH WRITE TO BE WELL

Now that you've learned the basic method of Step One: Write Your Stress Story, here's the example we've promised, which is Paul's Write to Be Well journal entries. Paul's writing demonstrates the basic use of the method after he experienced an acute health issue that forced him to move forward with his life, change his lifestyle, and manage his new, chronic condition. He chose to write over a period of six weeks in fifteen-minute increments.

With each step in the following three chapters, you will follow Paul's writing journey. Each step demonstrates how the basic method of Write to Be Well can be used. For starters, here is a quick summary of Paul.

Paul's Story

Paul was sixty-two when he had his heart attack. He's sixty-seven now and glad to be alive. Thankfully, his wife, Janie, was with him at the time. Her immediate call to 911 and the quick response of the ambulance and EMTs saved his life. He says, "The experience changed me forever." The memory of that warm summer day in July still haunts Paul—"the intense pain in my chest, radiating to my neck, jaw, arms, and back . . . the cold, clammy skin, the shortness of breath." He'd had no warning signs, just this sudden onslaught of gripping pain and panic. He was sure he was going to die. "It was a frightening experience to be so out of control."

Paul now refers to his life as having two phases—there's BHA (before heart attack) and AHA (after heart attack). BHA he had all kinds of unhealthy habits. He consistently worked twelve-hour days, ate junk food, and as he put it, "turned into a couch potato on my days off—sprawled out on the sofa with a beer and bag of chips by my side." He was exhausted all the time, stressed out, and overweight.

AHA, he's a different person. Today he's living a heart-healthy lifestyle. He walks at least a couple of miles every day and tries on most days to leave work after eight or eight and a half hours. He monitors his stress and eats balanced meals with protein, good fats, veggies, and fruit. When he doesn't pay attention to diet, exercise, and stress, he slips right back into his old patterns of being too busy to take care of himself.

Paul says, "The heart attack's been a hard lesson. One I hope never to repeat." He feels like he's been given a second chance at life. He wants to appreciate this gift by spending more time with his family, taking trips with his wife, checking off the items on his bucket list before he dies, and learning to say no when it's something he really doesn't want to do. Even so, it's a challenge. Paul's in a high-stress job that has demands from morning until night. He admits he is not at a point in his life when he would choose to make a major job change; with his writing, he is making the best of his situation.

Paul doesn't consider himself a writer, but he's been writing to-do lists, emails, and proposals his whole life. That makes him a writer! As a housing contractor, he says he needs to be super organized to keep the project moving forward, on budget, and on time. When he had his heart attack, he started using Write to Be Well to set a direction and learn to be accountable to himself and his health. He hoped that writing about the progress he'd be making toward living a healthy lifestyle would keep his goals front, center, and on target. As you read Paul's journal entries in this and the next three chapters, you will see how he uses Write to Be Well to support himself and what he values. In the following samples, Paul adheres to the guidelines for expressive writing by linking details of his heart attack to his emotions. He doesn't worry about grammar or style. He wrote for his eyes only until he decided he wanted us to share it.

Prompt One: Complete This Sentence Stem

The stressful situation (real or perceived) I am facing is . . .

I've been home from the hospital for two weeks. I'm grateful to be alive, but really pissed at myself for having this setback. I'm behind at work. There's a contract due and a house to finish. Not sure what's going on with the subcontractors. The phone's been ringing off the hook, and Janie is monitoring my calls. I know she means well, but I've got to get back to work. I tried to return some calls while still in the hospital, but the nurse fussed at me and eventually took away my phone. I felt like a child being reprimanded. My cardiologist has released me to work part-time, starting next week.

Prompt Two: Write Your Own Story

Write your story from the "I" perspective (first person), describing your thoughts and feelings surrounding the stressful situation, real or perceived.

I'm scared shitless! Sometimes when I think of that day, I feel a bit of panic. Can it happen again? Okay, I've had a heart attack. Lots of people do. But the doc told me part of my heart died that day. He said I had a widow-maker, 100 percent blockage in the left anterior descending artery. Thank God for Janie and her quick response. I know I scared her—hell, I scared myself. Our minister came to the hospital and asked if there was anything I wanted to talk about. That's when it hit me. I could die. Before that, it never crossed my mind. I didn't think I was dying. The girls came from Seattle and Atlanta to be with Janie and me. They were there in less than 24 hours. I get choked up when I think about it and the panic they must have felt. I was on my back for four days. When I got up for the first time, I couldn't walk. It took me a couple of days to regain enough strength. The cardiac rehab has been helpful and supportive. I really appreciate all the work they do on my behalf.

A week later, Paul wrote his story again. This time he felt compelled to go deeper into the details and emotions of what happened to him. The first time through, a burden was lifted, and he needed another burden to be lifted with the weight of the emotion he was feeling.

Here's my story, for the second time. That day will always be vivid. I was so calm and cool in the early stages of the heart attack. I'd just gotten out of the shower and had this strange feeling in my chest that I couldn't shake. It felt like I had indigestion and needed to belch. But I couldn't get it out. I told Janie I was calling 911. That I thought I might be having a heart attack. She insisted I sit down and took the phone from me. She dialed. The EMTs were at the house within minutes and quickly determined I was having a heart attack. They started treating me immediately. I was in the hospital within half an hour. I felt like a piece of meat—poked and prodded. I was in emergency one minute and the next thing I knew, I was out of surgery and in a hospital bed, wired up to IVs and god knows what else. Janie was always there and then the girls were by my side too. I was so disoriented. They had to tell me what happened. I'm scared thinking of it. Thankful too. So thankful that I'm alive. Now I'm feeling overwhelmed. I've been to cardiac rehab a couple of times and there is just so much to do—diet, exercise, etc. I need to make so many changes. How do I commit to this? For starters, I have to lose 30 pounds and walk every day. How am I going to do that??

Prompt Three: Shift Your Perspective

Now write your story from another person's point of view (third person).

Janie has been my rock. Here's what I think she would say about this whole experience. . . . Paul's been a decent patient. I know he's getting antsy to get back to his old routine, but things must change. He is so stressed about work. He tries to keep it to himself. But I can see how he handles it—a beer or two when he comes home. Not so bad in itself, but it leads to chips and peanuts. The doc says he needs to lose some weight and get on an exercise program. He's lost weight before, so he can do it. But when the stress escalates, he's back to his old habits.

The heart attack really scared me. I thought I was going to lose him. I felt like a zombie, just totally overwhelmed with doctors and medical discussions. Thank goodness the girls were there to hold my hand and guide the decision making. I'm grateful we have more years together. It makes me think about how we want to spend them. I love the guy and would do anything for him. I sure hope he makes a solid commitment to build heart-healthy habits.

Notes to Self: Reflection

The following questions are a guide for your reflection. Respond to those that are relevant to you in this moment.

1. What did you learn about yourself in responding to the prompts?
2. What did you notice about how stress plays out in your life? Did anything surprise you? Disappoint you? Annoy you? If so, be sure to name it!
3. What emotions did you uncover?
4. What happened in your body as you wrote? Did you experience any release of stress, or did you experience heightened anxiety?
5. Do you have clarity about the source of your stress, your thoughts, your feelings, and what they are "doing" to you? If not, you may want to go back and repeat the prompts.

I had a widow-maker and lived through it. I feel like the stars were aligned in my favor that day. Janie was by my side. The paramedics were at my house in minutes and knew exactly what to do. The cardiologist on duty is considered the best in the area. Everything fell into place. I'm alive and grateful!

It's been a hard couple of months. I cry more easily, especially when I think of my family and how they've supported me. I know they were scared too. I want to be part of their lives for years to come—family gatherings, grandchildren, travel, friends. I have a lot to live for.

I'm surprised at how emotional I feel when I write about that day. Heart attacks are serious, I know that. I don't want another one. I want to stay focused on a heart-healthy lifestyle. I still have a lot to give—and a lot to receive. It feels like a big challenge.

Commentary

Paul admits the body he once trusted suddenly and unexpectedly failed him. Writing about the heart attack, as Paul did, helped him name what happened. He called his heart attack a widow-maker. He knew it was serious. He wrote in detail about that day and linked the events to his emotional response. "I cry more easily." "I get choked up." "I could die." "Scared thinking about it." Expressing those feelings in writing helps Paul externalize his fears and worries in the privacy of his journal. No one else hears his confession. Being honest with his emotions diminishes their power over him and helps to release the pent-up stress associated with this traumatic event.

Paul's writing also indicates he has found meaning in the event. He acknowledges his family's support and love and shows gratitude for his life. He realizes he must make some lifestyle changes if he wants to live fully into the future.

If Paul were to continue writing about his heart attack, he might uncover more gems of understanding. However, he must decide when he is done. Going over the same details again and again can lead to rumination or circular thinking, which does not support a healthy perspective. Paul's writing shows he has identified the silver lining in this dark cloud. He's ready to go to the next step. Now on to the basics of Step Two, followed by the continuation of Paul's journal entries with Write to Be Well.

4

YOUR FUTURE

Picture It!

What might a life without stress look like for you? You might envision a subtle change, or a reinvention of your entire lifestyle. Whatever it is, there is no right or wrong choice. It is for you to decide what is most appropriate at this point in time.

In Step One you established a foundation and focused on the stress you identified as important to address. Now it's time to define what you want your future to look like and begin the journey to living that life. In Step Two you will identify what really matters to you. You then link this, what you value most, to your future vision and create an affirmation that boldly states your personal truth.

This second step of the Write to Be Well method uses affirmative writing, a style of writing that bridges the gap between where you are and where you want to be. By writing positively about your future, whether a goal, an event, or a way of living, you are setting an intention and stirring things up within yourself such that your brain actually takes action to help make it happen. This is neuroplasticity or the brain's ability to reorganize itself.[1]

In writing this affirmative, future statement, you might be thinking how Pollyanna it is to make a statement about the future that is enormously far from the ugly truth of the situation you are now in. An affirmation is not about denial; rather, it is a way to see the possibility of what can be and what you want to be, outside of your current state. In this way you can affirmatively set the goal for what you need and want to achieve and move yourself outside of the current mess you are living with!

Another emphasis within this step is what matters to you and your values. For substantive change to take place, whether a physical way of behaving or an attitude, linking your values to that need or desire to change is critical.

As an example, you might be stressed about your health, being over-weight and needing to lose weight. You've tried repeatedly with a variety of diets for years. Losing weight just doesn't happen, and you yo-yo back to being obese. You truly value the ability to get down on the floor and play with your kids, but then you have to get back up again! By naming and acknowledging what you value, from deep within yourself, the importance of a lifestyle change with your eating versus trying another diet will take on new meaning and support you in losing weight. The value, of course, needs to be linked to your affirmation. As you will learn in chapters 5 and 6, revisiting these values is enormously beneficial for you in Steps Three and Four.

To support you in identifying what matters and giving it a name, we provide a list of personal values in table 4.1 for your reference. You might also name some others of your own. With this being said, here we go with the how-to of Step Two, but first . . .

GUIDELINES FOR STEP TWO

Purpose: With this step you acknowledge your values and link them to your future vision as stated in your affirmation.

- **Contents:** This step has three writing prompts and three reflective writing questions.
- **Duration:** For Prompt One, take your time, maybe fifteen to thirty minutes, to review the list of personal values. Read through them, take your time to name the ones that initiate a reaction in you, and write a bit about them. Then move on to the prompt and complete it quickly. Remember, setting a timer can be helpful. Prompt Two is a fifteen-to-twenty-minute story-writing exercise that you can think of as a hybrid of expressive writing and affirma-

Personal Values

Accomplishment	Freedom	Preservation
Accountability	Friendship	Privacy
Accuracy	Frugality	Prosperity
Adventure	Fun	Punctuality
Appreciation	Global view	Quality of work
Beauty	Goodness	Regularity
Calm	Goodwill	Reliability
Challenge	Gratitude	Resourcefulness
Change	Hard work	Respect for others
Cleanliness	Harmony	Responsiveness
Collaboration	Holism	Results oriented
Commitment	Honesty	Rule of law
Communication	Honor	Safety
Community	Improvement	Satisfying other
Competence	Inclusion	Security
Competition	Independence	Self-reliance
Concern for others	Individuality	Service (to others, society)
Connection	Inner peace	Simplicity
Continuous improvement	Innovation	Skill
Cooperation	Integrity	Solving problems
Coordination	Intensity	Speed
Creativity	Justice	Spirit in life
Customer satisfaction	Kindness	Stability
Decisiveness	Knowledge	Standardization
Discipline	Leadership	Status
Discovery	Loving	Success
Diversity	Loyalty	Systemization
Ease of use	Maximum utilization	Teamwork
Efficient	Meaning	Timeliness
Enjoyment	Merit	Tolerance
Equality	Openness	Tradition
Excellence	Patriotism	Tranquility
Fairness	Peace	Trust
Faith	Perfection	Truth

Faithfulness	Personal growth	Unity
Family	Play	Variety
Family feeling	Pleasure	Wealth
Financial security	Power	Wisdom
Flair	Practicality	

tive writing. Be careful with your affirmation to choose positive words to express your future. Prompt Three may require twenty to thirty minutes to write your affirmation.

- **Frequency:** You can write over a period of two to three days or, if you choose, do it all in one sitting, for a total of about forty-five to sixty minutes.

- **Reminders:** This reflection is a quick one! It is a quick check-in and confirmation rather than a long dialogue of feedback with yourself. If your affirmation doesn't feel right, consider returning to the values list and your future story to see what needs a modification or confirmation. Please do follow the step-by-step guide on creating an affirmation, as the words you choose, and the way you state them, are proven to make a difference. The "Writing Guideline Summary" in the Section 2 introduction provides the general principles that are useful with all four Write to Be Well steps.

Now it is your turn to experience Step Two. The remainder of this chapter includes the Step Two instructions followed by Paul's example.

STEP TWO: AFFIRM YOUR STRESSLESS FUTURE

Prompt One: Identify What Matters

List three important values threatened by stress. Then insert each value into this sentence stem to test why it matters: What matters to me is ___ because ___ .

After reviewing the list of values in table 4.1, create a list that is most meaningful for you. Then, by considering the way the stress you are experiencing threatens what matters to you in the future, choose the three values that are most important.

Prompt Two: Write Your Future Story, Your Vision

> Write your future story, linking your values to your vision of life with reduced stress.

Now that you have named and explored the why of what matters most for you, write your story of what life looks like in the future by linking the values to your vision of the future and your life with reduced stress.

Write why you chose these values as they relate to your future life. Explain how they guide you to stay on course as you move forward. Your future story needs to touch on:

- What you want,
- What you strive for,
- How you feel, and
- What you've learned to support yourself in achieving the change you want.

Okay, ready to write? Go for it!

Prompt Three: Write Your Affirmation

> Create an "I" statement of what you want to do, be, or achieve in the future: I am . . .

Considering your future story and the values you've linked to it, it is time to write an affirmation to express what you want to do, be, or achieve. This is the goal you will be working with in Step Three. Before you begin, here are a few tips on writing an effective affirmation.

1. **Affirm only what you want.** Rather than writing, "I no longer have debt," write, "I owe nothing and am financially stable." Your affirmation names the change you want in your life. It intentionally affirms the qualities you wish to nurture.
2. **Make it believable.** Make your intention believable to you in the context of your future story. Express your affirmation by choosing positive words: "I am strong and energetic all day long after an invigorating twenty-minute morning walk."

3. **Write as if it's happening now.** Rather than writing, "I will take a walk every morning for twenty minutes," write your affirmation as, "I walk each day for twenty minutes." Write positively and express your affirmation in the present tense!

4. **Use language that supports a flourishing life filled with generativity. Avoid using any negative words such as *don't*, *can't*, *not*, or *try* , and *but* is simply not allowed!** Rather than writing, "I don't have the energy to exercise today," write instead, "Today I exercise because I am strong and healthy."

5. **Begin with gratitude.** Gratitude increases the power of the intention. "I am grateful for the smart decisions I made today."

6. **Deal immediately with negative self-talk.** As you write your affirmation, some of your doubts might pop into your head. Deal with them immediately. They are based on your old belief system, telling you this affirmation will never materialize. For example, you might write, "I am a wildly successful entrepreneur. My product just flies off the shelves." Meanwhile, inside your head, you hear yourself refuting this statement with thoughts like, "Oh, sure you are. You have bills up the kazoo and there's no way out of this financial morass." Stop your thoughts by dumping them on paper and counter them with the positive word that you want to be telling yourself.

Now write your one-sentence affirmation. Begin with "I am . . . ," "I feel . . . ," "I see . . . ," or any other "I" statement that is right for you.

Notes to Self: Reflection

The following three questions are a guide for your reflection. Respond now to those that are relevant to you in this moment.

1. Describe how your affirmation confirms your values and your desired future.
2. As you described your future story, name any emotions that arose and how they influenced you.
3. Are you ready to be guided in Step Three to write your plan to make your future a reality? If yes, you're ready to go. If no, revisit

your values, your future story, and your affirmation and modify as needed.

With this reflection, revisit the values you've named, your future story, and your affirmation. Be really honest in your writing; dig deeply into what you're feeling. Does your affirmation confirm your values and your desired future?

STEP TWO KEY ELEMENTS

This step builds on the foundation of your Step One *current state* to consider what really matters and what you want your future to be. The key elements of your writing with this step are that you have done the following:

- Identified the values that are most meaningful for you and linked them to your future story.
- Written as many details as you can to describe your future and the emotions you feel.
- Followed the guidelines for writing an effective affirmation that results in a succinct, positive statement as if you were already living with it in your stressless future.

PAUL'S STEP TWO JOURNEY WITH WRITE TO BE WELL

Paul's writing moves now from expressive writing to affirmative writing. This is where he cements his desire to live a heart-healthy lifestyle. His writing reminds him again why he wants to manage stress based on the values he has identified. Paul's writing reveals how his affirmation sets direction and guides him in making desired lifestyle changes.

Prompt One: Identify What Matters

List three important values threatened by stress.

It's been an overwhelming experience to figure out what I value. Then again, it's pretty easy too.

1. *Family*
2. *Integrity*
3. *Financial security*

What matters to me is __ because __ .

Okay, I will plug the words in and see what happens.

What matters to me is *family* because *I love them and know they love me. Life is rich, which I realized in a big way when they were by my side and supported me through the hard times with my heart attack. I had so many memories while lying there in the hospital. The years zipped through my mind and the richness of our family life. I love all my girls and would do anything in the world for them. I can't live without them. I want to create new memories as we grow old and the girls' lives unfold. I feel overwhelmed with love for them just thinking about the fact I could have lost out on the future with my family.*

Okay, number 2. What matters to me is *integrity* because *I am a man of my word. I am honest and forthright and I always live my life and my relationships according to moral principles. That sounds sort of righteous doesn't it? But yeah, I really do live with integrity. My work shows it. I know all too well being a general contractor that there are all kinds of ways I could shortchange the work, direct it to make more money, and not do the quality job I care about. I don't let that happen with my work. That's part of the reason I'm so damn busy—people know we do good work, stand by it, and are committed to doing it right. I have integrity with my work. Do I live with integrity in taking care of myself?*

Number 3. What matters to me is *financial security* because *I want to provide for my family. It's as simple as that! And I don't want us to have to live paycheck to paycheck like we did in the early years of our marriage. Growing up was scary. I didn't really understand what the finances were. Did they even call it that back then? I just know my parents worked awfully hard to provide the way they did for me and my sisters. They didn't have much for themselves later on. I've provided for my family and done a good job. I need to be sure we are secure in the future and, if God forbid I don't survive this, that Janie is ok financially.*

With work I have to admit I try to do more myself to make more money. I may need to hire some help. I've been doing the job of three people. Perhaps it's time to start training a job foreman. I've got to slow down with work and at the same time make sure we have financial security.

Prompt Two: Write Your Future Story, Your Vision

Write your future story, linking your values to your vision of life with reduced stress.

My future story—whoa—what is that? For starters, it's a life of no more heart attacks! Translation, good health and no surprises. I just finished writing about what matters. So, what does matter in the future? Good health, rich life with my loving family, being a man of my word, and us being able to enjoy life, not worrying about having enough money to do the things we need and want to do. My future story is Janie and I enjoying our lives together, visiting the girls, and loving life. That means me working for a while and figuring out how to transition to retirement. Whatever that is, we will figure it out together. It also means I will do what the doc tells me to be healthy. That's maintain my health by getting on and sticking to the diet they've recommended, adding an exercise regimen somehow to my weekly schedule. That's it too—I need to lighten the load at work by hiring someone I can trust to live up to the quality and ethics that I stand by. I can do it. I have to admit I feel stressed thinking about all the steps I need to take to make all this happen. I can do it by writing, exercising, and turning over some of my job tasks to a couple of new hires. Good hires. I have to start with my health 'cause without that—there's nothing. My family, my life, my work, and my financial security all depend on it. With the love and support of Janie, I know I will do this.

Prompt Three: Write Your Affirmation

Create an "I" statement of what you want to do, be, or achieve in the future: I am . . .

My affirmation: Today I am strong and healthy.

That's it! I said it. It's the root of all other things I want in my future. I'm going to write that down every day at the start of the day.

Notes to Self: Reflection

The following questions are a guide for your reflection. Respond to those that are relevant to you in this moment.

1. Describe how your affirmation confirms your values and your desired future
2. As you described your future story, name any emotions that arose and how they influenced you.
3. Are you ready to be guided in Step Three to write your plan to make your future a reality? If yes, you're ready to go. If no, revisit your values, your future story, and your affirmation and modify as needed.

I feel better after writing my affirmation. I sense a lightness in my spirit, not the heavy darkness I was feeling. Writing about my core values reminds me I'm a capable guy with an awesome family who still needs me around. They want me around! I don't want to be a victim of this heart attack. Restate that—I am not a victim of this heart attack. It was a tap on the shoulder or better yet a karate chop to the back of my head to wake up. I'll adjust my lifestyle to have a healthier diet and exercise. I'll monitor my stress and use writing as a way of taking inventory on how I'm doing. I'm pumped and ready to get started! It's real and I can feel this and will do this!

Commentary

Affirmative writing begins by naming what matters most to you. Paul selected *family*, *integrity*, and *financial security*. These are the core values that mean the most to him when he considers his current situation. In working with his core values, Paul reminds himself he doesn't have to make the changes alone—he has family who will support him. He recognizes and concedes he can hire staff to reduce the number of hours he spends at work, and by claiming himself as a man of integrity, Paul affirms his worth as a human being and builds ego strength. He can now openly receive the health information that he perceived earlier to be threatening to his current lifestyle.

By using words like *love, support, truth,* and *security,* Paul builds a positive framework for change. His language supports a flourishing life filled with generativity. Paul concludes this step with a strong, very simple statement affirming what he wants. "Today I am strong and healthy" sums it all up!

Now on to Step Three.

5

YOUR PLAN

Action Script It!

It is within your power to change your stress-filled narrative, your story, your mind-set, or your situation, and live the life you want. When you wrote your future story and affirmation in Step Two, you identified what you want your life to look like. When we see our future before us in a tangible way, as in writing, it gives us the drive and energy to do what it takes to realize our dream. Stating goals and having a realistic plan for the future you wish are keys for the journey to achieve your affirmation.

Action scripting is a writing process we have created where you combine actions and goals into a viable plan. Now, in this chapter, you will create your action plan. This plan could be as simple as one action item or have many items, depending on your stress situation. It's up to you to decide what helps you most to move forward! But first, a few words about goals and SMART goals.

Goal setting is recognized to provide direction and solidify a clear focus on what is important. For some, it provides motivation and a sense of purpose. When you think positively about what you have accomplished toward achieving a goal, no matter how large or small you view it, you develop a sense of control and satisfaction with each small step. Small steps are the best for sustaining movement toward success. SMART goals with small action steps in Step Three will support you in recognizing the positive emotions that lead you to success on your journey to greater well-being.

WHAT DOES SMART MEAN?

SMART is an acronym that you can use to guide your goal setting. Its criteria are commonly attributed to Peter Drucker's concept of "management by objectives." Success in achieving desired outcomes is proven to increase with the use of SMART.

To make sure your goals are clear and attainable, each one needs to be:

- **S**pecific (simple, sensible, significant),
- **M**easurable (meaningful, motivating),
- **A**chievable (agreed, attainable),
- **R**ealistic (reasonable, relevant and resourced, results based),
- **T**ime bound (time based, time limited, time/cost limited, timely, time sensitive).

HOW TO USE SMART

Specific

Your goal needs to be clear and specific. This will support you in focusing on what truly motivates you to achieve it. When drafting your goal, try to answer the five W questions:

- **What** do I want to accomplish?
- **Why** is this goal important?
- **Who** is involved?
- **Where** is it located?
- **Which** resources or limits are involved?

Example: Imagine you are currently stressed about your weight, and you'd like to overcome your yo-yo dieting. A specific, affirmative goal could be, "I will gain the skills and experience necessary to change my eating lifestyle forever and feel better."

Measurable

It's important to have measurable goals so you can track your progress and stay motivated. Assessing progress helps you to stay focused, meet your deadlines, and feel the excitement of getting closer to achieving your goal. Small measurable steps are best. Focus on each tiny item you have achieved, no matter how miniscule, rather than centering on a long list of what you have yet to do, as this can feel self-defeating!

A measurable goal needs to address questions such as these:

- How much?
- How many?
- How will I know when it is accomplished?

Example: You might measure your goal of acquiring the skills and experience needed to manage your weight and eating by consulting with a nutritionist and investing in some simple meal plan books within a two-week period.

Achievable

Your goal also needs to be realistic and attainable to be successful. In other words, it needs to stretch your abilities and still remain possible. When you set an achievable goal, you may be able to identify previously overlooked opportunities or resources that can bring you closer to it.

An achievable goal will usually answer questions such as these:

- How can I accomplish this goal?
- How realistic is the goal, based on other constraints, such as financial factors?

Example: You might need to ask yourself whether developing the skills required is realistic, based on your current situation. Do you have the time within the two-week period to meet with a nutritionist? Are the necessary resources available to you? Can you afford to do it?

Here's a tip for making goals achievable: beware of setting goals that someone else has exclusive power over. For example, making an appointment within the next two weeks might work for you, but not for the nutritionist. So before committing to your goal, you may need to do some homework and check out the viability of engaging people other than yourself.

Realistic

This aspect of SMART goal creation is about ensuring your goal matters to you, and that it also aligns with other related goals. We all need support and assistance in achieving our goals, but it's also important to retain control over them. Make sure your plans drive everyone forward, and that you're still responsible for achieving your own goal. A realistic goal can answer yes to these questions, which you will explore in your writing activities:

- Does this seem worthwhile?
- Is this the right time?
- Does this match other efforts and needs I have?
- Is it applicable in the current socioeconomic environment I am in?

Example: Is the upcoming two weeks the right time to undertake this? For example, is it the week before a huge deadline at work that you are accountable for? Can you clear some time on your calendar to do so? If yes, you are good to go! Otherwise, you might need to reconsider and modify the parameters you have set.

Time Bound

Every goal needs a target date. Some of us are procrastinators and perform best at the eleventh hour. Others of us need to begin immediately and have a metered approach to accomplishing a task. Reflect on your preferred approach and do what serves you best. This part of the SMART goal criteria helps to prevent everyday tasks from taking priority over longer-term goals.

A time-bound goal will usually answer these questions:

- When?
- What can I do six months from now?
- What can I do six weeks from now?
- What can I do today?

Example: By a certain date, I will research online meal-planning guides and browse Amazon books to find the resources I want to use.

GUIDELINES FOR STEP THREE

- **Purpose:** The purpose of this step is to define your action plan using SMART goals to achieve your desired future.
- **Contents:** This step has two writing prompts and two reflective writing questions to guide you in giving yourself feedback. It's been said that you always get the best answers when you talk to yourself. We've found some wisdom in that statement!
- **Duration:** Set aside thirty to sixty minutes to complete this step if your affirmation is a subtle change you desire to make. If your stress has many complex parts that need to be addressed one by one, then additional time may be needed. For the subtle change, under Prompt One, write for fifteen to thirty minutes. Prompt Two: spend fifteen to thirty minutes writing your SMART goals. If this is the very first time you've written SMART goals, be kind to yourself by using the step-by-step directions and examples. In time, SMART goals will become easy to define and may even become your preferred way to set goals.
- **Frequency:** It is best to complete the two prompts in Step Three in one writing session. Then take some time to step back and reflect on your area of focus and SMART goals before moving on to consider the reflective questions.
- **Reminders:** The SMART format provided in the instructions is important to follow until it becomes second nature for you. The "Writing Guideline Summary" in the introduction to Section 2 provides the general principles that are useful with all four Write to Be Well steps.

STEP THREE: PLAN TO UNRAVEL STRESS

Step Three uses your affirmation from Step Two as the starting point to express what you want your future to be. With Step Three, you define the action steps and SMART goal or goals you need to realize your affirmation. These goals and actions are your *plan*. For many of us, a plan can be very simple, while for others a plan may be one step of many. The key is that your plan should be meaningful to achieve *your* vision of the future.

Prompt One: Create Your Action Steps

> Write your affirmation from Step Two and create a list of the possible action steps you need for your affirmation to become a reality. Group like items, if any, and then assign a value of 1–5, with 5 being the highest priority.

After writing your affirmation, say it aloud and reflect on how it resonates with what you value. Think about the area within your affirmation that you've decided is your priority. Make a list of all the actions you might take to realize your affirmation. Be bold by brainstorming with yourself to write—scribbling is good too—all the thoughts and ideas that simply pop into your head, even those that might seem absurd. Take ten to fifteen minutes to work this prompt or up to thirty minutes if your affirmation is more complex.

With your brainstormed list, consider each action item to determine if it stands alone or might be grouped with others. Then ask yourself the degree to which it matters to you. You might want to do this by assigning a value of 1–5 next to each action item or group of action items, with 1 being least and 5 being most important. Next, choose the item or group from the list that is your priority for moving forward. What is the emotion you feel when you reevaluate your priority? Can you connect it with your story about the future and affirmation? If not, try repeating this process until you are satisfied with your response.

Prompt Two: Action Script Your SMART Goals

For your priority action, define your SMART goal by responding to the following sentence stems. It's okay to specify more than one goal; simply repeat the process.

- **Specific:** I will do . . .
- **Measurable:** I've achieved my goal when . . .
- **Achievable:** I will accomplish this by . . .
- **Realistic:** I will do this now because . . .
- **Time Bound:** I will complete this by . . .

Now it's time to write your SMART goal(s)—that is, specific, measurable, achievable, realistic, time bound—for the action item or grouping of action items you've identified. Together, these action items and goals become your action plan.

Example: This is from someone who is dealing with the financial stress of college tuition. His SMART goal was, "I will meet with a financial planner within two weeks to discuss how to pay for my son's college tuition."

- **Specific:** Meet with planner; discuss tuition issue (each of these came from the brainstormed list).
- **Measurable:** After the meeting, I'll have next steps to develop a strategy and plan to cover tuition payments for the next four years.
- **Achievable:** My schedule is clear, and the financial planner is available based on recent conversation.
- **Realistic:** My son is a year away from college, and I need a plan now.
- **Time Bound:** I have an appointment within two weeks.

Now it's your turn to action script the SMART goal(s) that corresponds with the action step or steps you plan to take. Think about the words you choose to express the action, being certain they are positive and actionable. You may have one goal or more than one. When you are first developing actionable goals, be kind to yourself and start with just three.

Notes to Self: Reflection

The following questions are a guide for your reflection. Respond to those that are relevant to you in this moment.

1. As I reflect on my goals, I (notice, think, feel, am surprised by, etc.) . . .
2. What do you hope will be the outcome of completing your goals?

Allow yourself at least a quick, five-minute break from your writing and the SMART goal or goals you've written. Then reread your action plan and reflect on these questions. Remember, written reflections are the way to provide yourself feedback.

Step Three Key Elements

Steps One and Two are the rock-solid foundation for this step. In Step One, you linked the details of actions and events with your emotions. You defined your stress as perhaps being totally stressed out, mildly tense, or having sensed it as an undercurrent of tension undermining your health. In Step Two, you identified your personal values, what really matters to you, and wrote a story of your vision of the future. The themes that you wrote about in Step Two are threads that carried over into Step Three, where you action scripted your plan to change something important to you and make it happen. Based on these layers of understanding, the key elements of Step Three are that you:

- Used positive words that energize, motivate, and direct what you do,
- Used strong action verbs,
- Defined the action steps that are meaningful for you,
- Prioritized your actions necessary to move forward,
- Created goals that are expressed SMARTly (i.e., specific, measurable, achievable, realistic, and time bound), and
- Formulated an action plan that you are ready to move forward with, no matter how big or small it is!

Wow! Congratulate yourself! Now more from Paul about his journey from ill health to a brighter future with Write to Be Well!

PAUL'S STEP THREE JOURNEY WITH WRITE TO BE WELL

Prompt One: Create Your Action Steps

Write your affirmation from Step Two and create a list of the possible action steps you need for your affirmation to become a reality. Group like items, if any, and then assign a value of 1–5, with 5 being the highest priority.

My affirmation: Today I am strong and healthy! Where do I begin? Actually, it's pretty clear. This reminds me a bit of doing a plan for a house reno and grouping things like the electrical, plumbing, and carpentry. I can do this. To be healthy I need to change my diet, exercise, and manage stress. Okay, here goes:

Diet (2):

- *no more fast food*
- *lay off the drive-through coffee*
- *reduce the unhealthy things like potato chips, French fries*
- *limit beer to one per night during week and two on Friday and Saturday*
- *increase veggies at dinner*
- *work fruit into my day—maybe a snack for work*
- *don't put extra salt on my food*
- *limit peanuts in favor of almonds, walnuts—I think that's what the nurse said*
- *add oatmeal to breakfast*
- *lose 20 pounds at least*

Exercise (3):

- *get one of those step counters*
- *take a walk after dinner*
- *go to the gym*
- *hire a personal coach*
- *join a spinning class*

- *park at the far end of the parking lot rather than up close to the door*
- *use the stairs not the elevator*
- *find an exercise buddy*
- *exercise at lunch*
- *prepare for a 5K run*
- *buy some new running shorts*

Stress (1):

- *keep a journal to monitor stress—they told me to do this*
- *do a stress check-in daily*
- *name stressors*
- *hire and train a job foreman*
- *take the MBSR (mindfulness-based stress reduction) class Janie told me about*
- *practice deep breathing when I feel anxious*
- *that gratitude journal thing—focus on the joy in life*
- *repeat my affirmation daily or more often—Today I am strong and healthy!*
- *take my vacation days*
- *leave work early when I can*
- *move, not coach potato, on the weekends*

I've highlighted three areas. Long lists for each. What do I work on first? They're all a priority. As far as my diet goes, the fruit option is a positive first step. The fast food—hmm—how do I get meals quickly? I know I need to eliminate some bad food choices, but I'll save those until later. Fruit is an easy place to start maybe, and I like fruit. Okay, the exercise thing. I'm already enjoying taking a walk after dinner with Janie. It gives us a chance to talk uninterrupted about our day and gets both of us off the couch. Granted, we could both lose some weight. This is how we can support each other and build a healthy habit together. Stress, that's a tough one. For starters, maybe I can get into the habit of a daily stress check-in like they talked to me about. I'm learning how to listen to my body. I check in with my gut and my head. When I'm stressed, my stomach is in a knot and my forehead feels tight. Naming the stress and writing about it has helped me start to release the tension. I can figure out how to deal with it. Just thinking about it doesn't work for me. This writing's becoming a problem-solving method to help me manage my stress. I feel like my stress is the king of priorities and greater than a 5! Okay, this is where I need to start and then I won't feel as stressed about the diet stuff and exercise. The one area I need and want to start focusing on now is stress management!!!!! One thing at a time, don't stress myself out. Small steps. Don't get overwhelmed. I am learning. One goal to start. I can do this.

Prompt Two: Action Script Your SMART Goals

For your priority action, define your SMART goal by responding to the following sentence stems. It's okay to specify more than one goal; simply repeat the process.

- *Specific: I will do a stress check-in with myself each day at noon.*
- *Measurable: I will use a 1–5 scale; 5 is BAD.*
- *Achievable: Yes, I will make the time—only take a few minutes out of my day.*
- *Realistic: Yes and no. I can do the check-in, but then what do I do with it?*
- *Timebound: Complete my stress check-in daily with a minimum of every other day.*

Notes to Self: Reflection

The following questions are a guide for your reflection. Respond to those that are relevant to you in this moment.

1. As I reflect on my goals, I (notice, think, feel, am surprised by, etc.) . . .
2. What do you hope will be the outcome of completing your goals?

Yes, I recognize that I am ready. Taking this first small step feels good and right to be starting with stress management. Yes, it's important. Hell, they've told me it's the crux of my heart issue. I'm not sure I can do this though. I see a big problem. What do I do if my stress is at a level 5? I can't just ignore it! Okay, I can tie it to exercise. That's what I'll do. I need another goal.

SMART goal 2:

- **Specific:** *If my stress level is 4 or greater, I will spend 10 additional minutes first closing my eyes and taking a deep breath, then taking a break from whatever I am doing by moving—taking a walk, doing a flight of stairs, or excusing myself from the situation I am in temporarily.*
- **Measurable:** *I will keep a log of stress levels and the action I took on my phone—in Notes.*
- **Achievable:** *Yes, I can do this! I know I need to take more breaks throughout my day.*
- **Realistic:** *Yes, using the stairs, going outside, and taking a deep breath work for me.*
- **Timebound:** *I can spare 10 minutes in the day to manage my stress, multiple times if necessary. The tradeoff if not is my health and my life.*

Yes, okay, I can make this happen. I know I can, and I will. Hell, it's a bit like when the girls were first born. I had no idea or confidence in being a dad. I did it. I learned. They mattered then and matter now. I can do this. One small step at a time.

Commentary

Chapter 2 points out that people with plans and goals have a greater chance for success than people without them. And a written plan with SMART goals keeps you focused, motivated, and energized. Paul has a small, solid plan to do two simple things to manage his stress. He started with a random list of many actionable items, narrowed it to a few, and then chose one action item to start with. He can now work his specific stress management goals until he feels comfortable with them and later add more goals to focus on diet, exercise, or other issues. In this manner, he manages the change in his life without being overwhelmed. By writing his SMART goals, Paul can refer to them as often as he wants to remind himself of his commitment. Written goals increase his chance for success. In time, he will make it happen—one SMART goal at a time! He also linked the confidence factor to his love for his family, which is one of his key values. The fact that he thought of gaining confidence as a dad when his girls were babies and linked it to his challenge now to gain confidence in managing stress is enormously supportive to his ability to develop new stress management habits. He recognizes he did it before and will do it again!

Now on to Step Four.

6

YOUR LIFE

Get Well, Be Well!

The steps in Write to Be Well provide a foundation and map for you to discover your future vision, affirm your personal truth, and create an action plan for taming the tension in your life and managing stress on your journey to optimal health and well-being. Through the previous three steps, you have created a personalized plan to move forward with a priority area of your life. This is a starting point, and you have identified what you have chosen as the best action at this point in time to move forward. It might be large or small. It needs to be what is right and meaningful for you and what you value in life.

Step Four prepares you for enacting your plan. It is the final step in the process that launches you into a lifestyle of managing the priorities that matter. You may choose to initiate a big change or make subtle differences in behavior. You also might choose to maintain the status quo in a new and different way. Using the writing tools you have learned thus far, the important insight Step Four helps you to uncover is found in your responses to the following questions:

- Are you ready to move forward?
- Are you confident in your ability to do so?
- Is it important for you to enact your plan?
- Do you believe that you can do this?

- What is your attitude toward making the changes you've identified in your action plan?
- How will you hold yourself accountable?

Step Four leverages the power of reflective writing to explore the very questions posed above. Reflective writing helps you gain a deeper understanding of yourself by exploring and discovering why you need or want to make a change. Writing reflectively supports you in expressing your beliefs, doubts, and concerns and, most importantly, in determining whether you are truly committed to enacting your plan and achieving your goals.

In chapter 2 we noted the quote, "If you change the way you look at things, the things you look at change."[1] The reflective writing you do in this step is the very way to help you shift the view of what you are facing. An *aha* we frequently hear from clients challenged with the stress of needing to lose weight is that it is not really about finding the right diet and sticking to it for a period of time. Instead, through reflective writing, they realize they don't need to go on another *diet* at all; rather, with their shift in perspective, they set their sights on achieving a lifestyle of eating what is best for them. This often happens after connecting with the values that they hold most dear. Now here are the basics of Step Four to get well and be well.

GUIDELINES FOR STEP FOUR

- **Purpose:** The heart of this step is reflecting on the growth and change you want to achieve by assessing your perceived competence to make it happen, your readiness, and being honest with yourself about your level of commitment as it relates to what you value most in life.
- **Contents:** This step has three writing prompts and a brief reflection.
- **Duration:** After briefly reviewing your plan, write for fifteen to twenty minutes in response to Prompt One. Prompt Two requires another fifteen to twenty minutes of reflective writing. By Prompt Three, the words will flow from your pen, pencil, or fingertips. Expect to spend twenty minutes on this prompt.

- **Frequency:** We suggest this step be completed in one writing session for a total of about forty-five to sixty minutes.
- **Reminders:** Remember that grammar, punctuation, and the like are not important here. What you write is for you to cherish and use to support yourself in your journey to optimal health. The "Writing Guideline Summary" in the Section 2 introduction provides the general principles useful with all four Write to Be Well steps.

STEP FOUR: REFLECT AND COMMIT TO DESTRESS

Step Four is pivotal in that you move on to a lifestyle of writing to support yourself as you enact your plan and achieve your goals. The question is, are you equipped for the journey? The prompts in Step Four are designed for you to explore your readiness, competence, and commitment.

Prompt One: Explore Your Readiness

Write in response to one or more of these questions to assess your willingness, belief, and commitment to move forward.

1. Are you confident in your ability to move forward? If yes, move on. If not, what do you need to feel more confident?
2. On a scale of 1 to 5, with 5 being the most important, how important is it for you to enact your plan? If a 4 or 5, move on, and if less than 4 or 5, explore why.
3. What do you believe about yourself and your ability to do this? Write it down; then dig deeply to explore if this belief holds true. If not, change it to reflect your inner truth.
4. Describe your attitude toward making the changes you've identified in your action plan. For example, are you pumped and ready to go, fearful, or . . . ?
5. Describe how you will hold yourself accountable. How will you reward yourself?

Prompt One includes a complete list of questions to challenge your state of readiness.

Once you've mastered the prompts in this step, you may choose to use these questions as guidance and simply summarize your response. You will see in Section 3 the stories of other people who have used Write to Be Well as a guide rather than responding with a written response to each question. This is what we refer to as the scalability and flexibility of the method.

Prompt Two: Reflect on Your Plan

Write a letter to a trusted person and describe the following:

- What you're going to do (action plan),
- What you've learned about yourself to make it happen,
- Why you're committed,
- Any obstacles that may arise,
- What you will do about them.

This trusted person could be a friend, family member, colleague, or someone imaginary. What's important is that the person is someone you would feel comfortable expressing your deepest feelings of commitment to. You don't have to mail this letter unless you want to share it. You simply write it down and by doing so examine your commitment and what really matters to you. Dump the words on the page and let the emotions flow!

Prompt Three: Contract for Change

Create a contract with yourself that positively states the key elements of your letter. Sign it, date it, and refer to it every day.

When you create this contract, include reminders of what you will gain and ways you will maintain momentum when obstacles emerge. Include a list to acknowledge your successes and how you will contract with yourself to reward your progress. Also note any adjustments to your plan as you proceed and what you will do to keep the momentum going.

Notes to Self: Reflection

Reflect and write about what you are proudest of right now! Take a few moments to think about the progress you've made with Write to Be Well. You deserve to congratulate yourself. You now have a plan of action and way forward with what matters to you most, whether large or small. Acknowledge your achievement by writing about what you're the proudest of at this point.

STEP FOUR KEY ELEMENTS

The key elements of Step Four to pay attention to are the words you use to unlock the understanding you have of your readiness, competence, and commitment to change your situation.

Scan your words and check for the use of causal words as described in chapter 2. They will assist you in the process of unlocking your beliefs about yourself and shifting your perspective. Examples of causal words are *cause*, *effect*, and *reason*. Look for the relationship you have expressed, the *whys* behind your commitment and contract with yourself.

Next scan for words that provide positivity and insight about your perspective and attitude about yourself. Check to see how often these words are part of your new vocabulary. Have you expressed

- **Being worthy?** By realizing your self-worth, you can energize yourself to face whatever obstacle you encounter. Don't lose sight of the fact you are worthy of respect and need not compare yourself to others and what they do or say about you, themselves, or others.
- **Having courage?** Have you indicated the courage you feel with your plan and commitment? Write to Be Well offers you opportunities to do anything you have your heart and mind set to do, even the things that frighten you.
- **That you are enough?** Have you gained the insight that whatever you need you can find within yourself? You have enough to make it happen. While there is always room to improve, consider your self-worth and remind yourself that you have the skills and competence to do so, if you take one step forward at a time.

- **Gratitude?** Have you acknowledged all that you have and can do with gratitude? Often, we focus so much on stress and the bad things that are going on in our lives that we forget all the beautiful things we have in life and to be grateful for them.
- **Focus?** By using the reflective and affirmative writing skills you have learned, focus on your goals and on positive things; avoid concentrating on things that will keep you from reaching your goals and people whose intentions may prove to be an obstacle.
- **Your self-image as a warrior?** Is your commitment that of a warrior? What self-image is reflected in your writing? Know that through the journey, things can be viewed as neither good nor bad; they are simply challenges a warrior continues to address by saying, "I am strong," and asking, "What am I going to do about it?"
- **Your desire to live?** The realization that life is short serves as an inspiration to be creative, seek and learn new things, and live life to the fullest.
- **Believing?** Does your letter of commitment show the belief you have in yourself that you won't quit? Look for these and similar words that you have used to unlock the meaning you've found in taking action to change your personal stress, whatever it may be, and live your life without tension.

PAUL'S STEP FOUR JOURNEY WITH WRITE TO BE WELL

Paul has shared that he frequently reads, and rereads, what he has written. He finds it to be an inspiration to keep going and tackle another area of his life where he needs to make a change or improve what he is currently working on. Here are his responses to questions about readiness after rereading all his first-time responses from Steps One, Two, and Three.

Prompt One: Explore Your Readiness

Write in response to one or more of these questions to assess your willingness, belief, and commitment to move forward.

- Are you confident in your ability to move forward? If yes, move on. If not, what do you need to feel more confident? *Yes, I am because I've spilled my guts writing honestly. I can do this.*
- On a scale of 1 to 5, with 5 being the most important, how important is it for you to enact your plan? If a 4 or 5, move on, and if less than 4 or 5, explore why? *Okay, this is a 5+++. I choose to live and get healthy. I care about Janie, the girls, what I stand for as a person, my work, and providing for my family.*
- What do you believe about yourself and your ability to do this? Write it down, then dig deep to explore if this belief holds true. If not, change it to reflect your inner truth. *I can do this. One small step at a time. This first thing isn't huge. It's a start. I can. I will. I must. I want to.*
- Describe your attitude toward making the changes you've identified in your action plan. For example, are you pumped and ready to go, fearful, or . . . ? *Motivated despite sometimes feeling down and tired.*
- Describe how you will hold yourself accountable. How will you reward yourself? *I am sharing all this with Janie. I have to do it myself and I asked her to let me simply share with her how I am doing. My reward will be taking an afternoon off and a date with Janie.*

Prompt Two: Reflect on Your Plan

Write a letter to a trusted person and describe the following:

- What you're going to do (action plan),
- What you've learned about yourself to make it happen,
- Why you're committed,
- Any obstacles that may arise,
- What you will do about them.

Dear Janie, Maria, and Jenn,

This heart attack has really thrown me off balance. I'm truly grateful for all the love and support you've given me throughout this ordeal. I realize again how much you all mean to me and how important our family is in my life. It is what I value the most. I'm thankful to be alive and ready to share many more life adventures with you. I know I need to get my act together and focus on my health. I can do this! I know it!

There are steps I plan to take to live a heart-healthy lifestyle. I confess you've been nagging me about some of this stuff for years and I've ignored you with hundreds of excuses. But I'm ready to make some changes. Over the last few weeks, I've been reading all the information the cardiologist gave me. I've decided to focus on three key areas: stress, diet, and exercise. I've come up with a first-step plan and goals and written it all down. I want to post it on the bathroom mirror and look at it every morning as a reminder.

I have a lot of changes to make, but I want to avoid being overwhelmed with too much all at once. So I'm going to tackle one thing at a time. I've decided to start with stress management since the doctor has emphasized that smoking and stress are proven links to heart disease. I've designed a stress check-in to monitor how I'm feeling throughout the day, and when my stress is high, I have a plan for managing it. Once I get into this routine, I'll dive into diet and exercise.

I want you to know I'm in this for the long haul. I want to feel better and be alive! I want to trust my body again. But I especially want to be around to spend time with each of you. I love you.

Love, Paul/Dad

Prompt Three: Contract for Change

Create a contract with yourself that positively states the key elements of your letter. Sign it, date it, and refer to it every day.

Starting my own business has been one of my most difficult life journeys. I can still remember the early days when it was just me and I contracted with plumbers, electricians, and carpenters to get the job done. Cash flow was a big issue. I worked long hours and always came home tired and dirty—head to toe! I'm proud of myself for sticking it out. Over the past 20 years, I've created a business with a good reputation for producing a quality house. I don't give up easily. I know I'm tenacious and strong willed. I can push through the tough times, but not anymore at the expense of my health. I've had help building this business. I've consulted with lawyers, accountants, other building contractors, and experts in management. Of course, Janie's been my biggest cheerleader and sounding board. When I'm dealing with difficult issues, she's always been there to listen and encourage me.

So how can I apply what I've learned from building a business to my current situation? I know I'm determined when I set my mind to it. Writing down my SMART goals puts my action plan front and center. I want to make these lifestyle changes, but I'm not going to drive myself as hard as I did when I was young—it'll just create more stress. The challenge will be to pace myself and implement the changes one step at a time. I'm open to calling on the experts to help me. I've never worked with a dietician or personal coach, but I'm willing to seek their advice. I like my cardiologist and I know the hospital has all kinds of classes for cardiac patients. When I share my goals with Janie, she'll stand by my side. She said she would. I believe and will make these changes last for the duration of my life—I just need to be patient with myself!

Here's my contract with myself!

I, Paul, promise myself that I will implement this plan, which outlines the lifestyle changes I want to improve my health and well-being. I'm starting with stress management and then addressing diet and exercise. I still have a lot of living to do. I want to spend my time with my family, travel, and enjoy whatever opportunities life affords me.

When obstacles emerge, I will:

- revisit my goals and tweak them as necessary
- not hesitate to use the professionals who can help me stay on track
- ask Janie to be my cheerleader and encourage me to keep going
- keep writing, expressing myself, and setting up the next step to move forward rather than stuffing it all inside and ignoring what matters to me

I affirm: Today I am strong and healthy! I look forward to the day when I can say that with conviction and move on to my next affirmation.

Signed: Paul. Dated: May 25.

Notes to Self: Reflection

Today, I'm a different man. The heart attack changed my life! It knocked me down physically and emotionally about as low as I've ever been. I felt weak, not only in body, but as a man. I couldn't fulfill my responsibilities to my family, my job, or even myself. I'm glad I've been *writing about that day and all the mixed feelings I've had. This dark cloud has finally lifted and I'm feeling much stronger and in control now. I have a plan and a way forward. I am most proud of my positive attitude and my renewed hope in a future with me in it!*

Commentary

Paul completed the four steps of Write to Be Well over the course of six weeks. Step Four asks him to reflect on how far he's come and what he's learned since those early days of his heart attack. He chooses to write a letter to his family, but he could have written to a trusted friend or even a private letter to God. He will decide whether he wants to share the letter with anyone. The act of writing a summary of his learnings reinforces his commitment to live a heart-healthy lifestyle. His letter includes specifics about his plan and acknowledges his core value of family. He can look back on this letter weeks later to remind himself what he learned, what he's committed to, and what he values.

In the second prompt, Paul reflects on a life challenge from his past and names the personal attributes that sustained him during this difficult time. The goal here is to apply those same strengths, beliefs, and resources to his new challenge. Paul's journal entry demonstrates he understands how to link past success with future success. He ends on a positive note, but acknowledges change takes time, patience, and fortitude!

Finally, Paul writes, signs, and dates a contract with himself. Once again, this is a summary of his commitment to change and addresses what he will do when obstacles emerge. Like his letter, Paul can refer to his contract as often as he wants. By writing it down, his words become agents of transformation and a catalyst for the change he envisions. Both documents are designed to help him stay motivated, energized, and focused on the prize—the heart-healthy lifestyle he desires.

IN SUMMARY

Provided here for your future use is a summary of the Write to Be Well four steps and writing prompts.

STEP ONE: WRITE YOUR STRESS STORY

Prompt One: Complete This Sentence Stem

The stressful situation (real or perceived) I am facing is . . .

Prompt Two: Write Your Own Story

Write your story from the "I" perspective (first person), describing your thoughts and feelings surrounding the stressful situation, real or perceived.

Prompt Three: Shift Your Perspective

Now write your story from another person's point of view (third person).

Notes to Self: Reflection

The following questions are a guide for your writing. Respond to those that are relevant to you in this moment.

1. What did you learn about yourself in responding to the prompts?
2. What did you notice about how stress plays out in your life? Did anything surprise you? Disappoint you? Annoy you? If so, be sure to name it!
3. What emotions did you uncover?
4. What happened in your body as you wrote? Did you experience any release of stress, or did you experience heightened anxiety?
5. Do you have clarity about the source of your stress, your thoughts, your feelings, and what they are "doing" to you? If not, you may want to go back and repeat the prompts.

STEP TWO: AFFIRM YOUR STRESSLESS FUTURE

Prompt One: Identify What Matters

List three important values threatened by stress. Then insert each value into this sentence stem to test why it matters: What matters to me is __ because __ .

Prompt Two: Write Your Future Story, Your Vision

Write your future story, linking your values to your vision of life with reduced stress.

Prompt Three: Write Your Affirmation

Create an "I" statement of what you want to do, be, or achieve in the future: I am . . .

Notes to Self: Reflection

The following three questions are a guide for your reflection. Respond to those that are relevant to you in this moment.

1. Describe how your affirmation confirms your values and your desired future.
2. As you described your future story, name any emotions that arose and how they influenced you.
3. Are you ready to be guided in Step Three to write your plan to make your future a reality? If yes, you're ready to go. If no, revisit your values, your future story, and your affirmation and modify as needed.

STEP THREE: PLAN TO UNRAVEL STRESS

Prompt One: Create Your Action Steps

Write your affirmation from Step Two and create a list of the possible action steps you need for your affirmation to become a reality. Group like items, if any, and then assign a value of 1–5, with 5 being the highest priority.

Prompt Two: Action Script Your SMART Goals

For your priority action, define your SMART goal by responding to the following sentence stems. It's okay to specify more than one goal; simply repeat the process.

- **Specific:** I will do . . .
- **Measurable:** I've achieved my goal when . . .
- **Achievable:** I will accomplish this by . . .
- **Realistic:** I will do this now because . . .
- **Time Bound:** I will complete this by . . .

Notes to Self: Reflection

The following questions are a guide for your reflection. Respond to those that are relevant to you in this moment.

1. As I reflect on my goals, I (notice, think, feel, am surprised by, etc.) . . .
2. What do you hope will be the outcome of completing your goals?

STEP FOUR: REFLECT AND COMMIT TO DESTRESS

Prompt One: Explore Your Readiness

Write in response to one or more of these questions to assess your willingness, belief, and commitment to move forward.

1. Are you confident in your ability to move forward? If yes, move on. If not, what do you need to feel more confident?

2. On a scale of 1 to 5, with 5 being the most important, how important is it for you to enact your plan? If a 4 or 5, move on, and if less than 4 or 5, explore why.

3. What do you believe about yourself and your ability to do this? Write it down; then dig deeply to explore if this belief holds true. If not, change it to reflect your inner truth.

4. Describe your attitude toward making the changes you've identified in your action plan. For example, are you pumped and ready to go, fearful, or . . . ?

5. Describe how you will hold yourself accountable. How will you reward yourself?

Prompt Two: Reflect on Your Plan

Write a letter to a trusted person and describe the following:

- What you're going to do (action plan),
- What you've learned about yourself to make it happen,
- Why you're committed,
- Any obstacles that may arise,
- What you will do about them.

Prompt Three: Contract for Change

Create a contract with yourself that positively states the key elements of your letter. Sign it, date it, and refer to it every day.

Notes to Self: Reflection

Reflect and write about what you are proudest of right now!

Section 3

The Art of Living
Case Studies

What does it mean to live well? What role does health play in living a good life? Do we have control over our lifestyle? These are some of the questions we asked ourselves and others as we began to shape Write to Be Well into a writing method that would help others. In our experiences of sharing writing with our clients in counseling, coaching, and business settings, we found answers to our questions. They told us the Write to Be Well method helped them name life stressors so they could work with them, make the behavioral changes they wanted, and renew their commitment to living a healthy, vibrant life. Their writing facilitated relief from past wounds and opened new avenues for change.

In the chapters ahead, you'll meet four actual people, with fictitious names, who granted us use of their stories. Each person used Write to Be Well to manage the stress associated with major life challenges and their everyday stress. In their journal pages, their writing is natural, authentic, flow-of-consciousness writing. As our "Writing Guideline Summary" suggests, they did not need to concern themselves about syntax and grammar, spelling, punctuation, or run-on sentences. We didn't change their writing unless required for clarity. Their writing shows how context and feelings are more important than writing style with Write to Be Well.

In their journal entries, you'll see that each person used Write to Be Well a bit differently. They all began by responding to all the prompts in each step; then, as they became more familiar with the method, they took shortcuts, responding only to the prompts that were most relevant to their current situation and time constraints.

Their use of Write to Be Well demonstrates the scalability (little problem or big problem) and flexibility (shortcuts, as described above) of this method. If a prompt stimulated lots of thoughts and feelings, they wrote pages; at other times, they wrote a brief sentence or even a few words. Some even chose to jot down notes on a paper napkin. In all cases, they followed the four-step method—one, two, three, four! Write to Be Well is an integrated system, with each step leading logically to the next. It's important to follow the sequence. Once you learn the four steps, you'll find it's user-friendly!

In the pages ahead, you'll read the journal entries from Logan, a graphic artist, who writes to focus on what he needs to do to manage a job change; Amy, a single mom, who writes to handle the stress of dealing with her ex; Yvonne, newly diagnosed with diabetes, who finds writing helps her manage her chronic condition; and Warren, who writes to grieve the death of his wife of thirty-nine years and in the process discovers there is life after loss.

Our commentary on the journal entries follows each of the steps. It highlights how the different types of writing—expressive, affirmative, action scripting, and reflective—support the writers' stories, leading them closer in each entry to understanding their situation and what to do about it. We also comment on how the writers responded to a prompt, including what their word choice and story line reveal about their thoughts and emotions. Our hope is that you will learn from their writing experiences and use the comments to guide you in your responses.

7

CAREER QUANDARY

Logan started using Write to Be Well six months ago to sort out his dilemma with his job. He's a self-employed graphic artist whose business has evolved into an area he no longer enjoys because it conflicts with his core values. Logan acknowledges that direct-mail marketing brochures, catalogs, and newsletters pay the bills, but he is an environmentalist who doesn't want his creative products to fill rivers, streams, and landfills with what he considers junk mail. He'd prefer to be a good steward of resources and use his creative talents to teach children about caring for the environment. He volunteers now with an amateur acting troupe that performs at various libraries and churches. Logan designs the sets and costumes, and he helps with the scripts. This work energizes him. He'd like to find a way to take the environmental message to a larger audience of children and do it as a full-time paying job. He's toying with the idea of starting a cartoon strip and trying to syndicate it.

Logan decided to use Write to Be Well to manage his stress and redirect his business model to be more in keeping with his values. He hoped the writing would help him stay focused and disciplined as he explored ways to make this transition. The first time he used Write to Be Well, Logan followed the guidelines, did all the writing prompts, and answered all the questions. But as he continued to write using the four-step Write to Be Well method, he fine-tuned his process and wrote to all four steps in fifteen minutes or less. He likened his writing practice to "muscle memory," adding, "Once I learned the steps, it was easy for me to write just a few sentences to stay focused on my goals for the day."

Logan's experience with Write to Be Well demonstrates the flexibility of the method. He's written to the same prompts multiple times and says, "I don't mind doing the same prompts over and over. Each time I address something slightly different. Writing it down helps me clear away all the distractions and focus on my main goal. Each time I write, I go deeper into my thoughts, feelings, options, and plans."

Logan shares his writing to illustrate the evolution of his thinking and how writing has helped him manage his stress and sort through his opportunities. He admits he still hasn't resolved his job dilemma, but he's making progress one SMART goal at a time!

Here's his first go-round with Write to Be Well. This time through, he writes to all the prompts. From Logan's journal . . .

ROUND ONE OF WRITE TO BE WELL

Step One: Write Your Stress Story

Prompt One: Complete This Sentence Stem

The stressful situation (real or perceived) I am facing is *I create marketing trash and promote consumption of plastic!*

Prompt Two: Write Your Own Story

Write your story from the "I" perspective (first person), describing your thoughts and feelings surrounding the stressful situation, real or perceived.

I spend 8 to 10 hours of my day creating art that conflicts with my core value of stewardship. Example—My client Sheila uses a ton of plastic to package her homemade salsa. It's mind-blowing! Yes, the ingredients are all organic and delicious; yet, the plastic she packages her salsa in just ruins its homemade value. I know she needs to sell her product using the most cost-effective packaging, but I want it to be environmentally friendly.

My job needs to support my values. This is becoming a problem for me. Every time I put a direct-mail marketing package together, I feel like I'm selling out to the establishment. It's hard for me to promote myself when I don't really believe in what I'm doing. As a business owner, I'm not accountable to anyone other than myself. But my income is tanking! I've got to get a grip on this problem.

I know what I want to do, but I don't know if it's possible. I've been sketching cartoon characters for years. I want to create scripts for these characters that teach children about the environment. Then maybe I can create puppets to deliver the same messages. Artists like Jim Henson and Charles Schultz are my role models. I love the Muppets and Snoopy. The characters are fun! Both men turned their dreams into a highly profitable business. I'd like to use my creative talent for something good. Not doing so is sucking the energy and life out of me. I don't know how to make the shift from graphic artist to cartoonist, much less how to generate the income I need to pay the bills!

Prompt Two: Write Your Own Story (Again)

Logan decides to dig deeper into his story, so he repeats Prompt Two, taking a different approach here than in his first story.

I grew up on a 40-acre farm in northern Iowa. Dad grew corn and soybeans. Our house was isolated, so I spent a lot of time by myself. I loved reading and drawing. I had a weird little character I drew called Al. He was cartoonish with a fat, round belly and big feet. Al was a wise man though. He loved the trees, flowers, streams, and all of nature. He was a little like Paul Bunyan—an early environmentalist.

I guess Dad was an environmentalist too. He was one of the earliest organic farmers. He valued the land and didn't want to do anything to pollute it. He didn't use pesticides; he rotated his fields and allowed two to lie fallow every year. I grew up learning about caring for all resources.

I just can't stand what I'm doing now. I'm afraid my beautiful packaging is ending up in a landfill or getting dumped into streams and oceans. It makes me sick! I've got to get out of this business. But how?

A teacher recently invited me to her classroom to do some cartooning. I had so much fun with my big easel and magic markers. It was easy to engage the children with my animal characters and their esca-

pades into the woods. I could be silly with them. I had the characters doing all kinds of nasty things in the woods—like spitting out chewing gum into a pile of leaves and dropping their trash along the path. The kids really got involved in the story, shouting out answers or booing when the characters made a mistake. The teacher suggested I apply for a county grant to perform in the schools. It's a good lead. I'll follow up on it. Maybe I can be an artist-in-residence and get paid by the county.

Prompt Three: Shift Your Perspective

Now write your story from another person's point of view (third person).

This is from a client's perspective:

Logan does great work! My salsas and chips really stand out at our crowded farmers' market. The packaging is colorful and he's developed a logo for me with a cartoonish Chihuahua that says the funniest things. I think people buy the product because the packaging is so darn cute!

Logan's prices are reasonable and he always delivers the artwork on time. Also, he makes the printing arrangements. That gives me more time to make my salsa and chips. He has been grumbling a bit lately about the packaging—something to do with the plastic container I use for my salsa. I don't know what he expects me to do about it. It's the least expensive way to package this product and keep an eye on my profit margin. He says it has something to do with the environment, concern about pollution. Well, that's not my problem!

Notes to Self: Reflection

The following questions are a guide for your writing. Respond to those that are relevant to you in this moment.

1. What did you learn about yourself in responding to the prompts?
2. What did you notice about how stress plays out in your life? Did anything surprise you? Disappoint you? Annoy you? If so, be sure to name it!
3. What emotions did you uncover?
4. What happened in your body as you wrote? Did you experience any release of stress, or did you experience heightened anxiety?

5. Do you have clarity about the source of your stress, your thoughts, your feelings, and what they are "doing" to you? If not, you may want to go back and repeat the prompts.

As I read over this, I can see I have a major conflict! It's eating away at my enthusiasm for going to work. I'm in a funk and I need to get out of it. If I could just find a way to use my art in ways that align with my values, I'd be a much happier person.

My writing sounds so negative. I'm complaining and whining. That's not me. I'm usually positive and upbeat. I need to build time into my schedule to explore some other artistic opportunities, especially those that support my values. I know myself. When I'm not being creative, I'm in a funk. I think my clients can tell when I'm flat. I'd better be careful or I could lose them—and then, what would I do?

Commentary

Logan's writing reveals good understanding of his situation. He identifies his stress as the conflict he feels between what he does for a living and his values. He enriches his story by referencing his dad's love of the land and how, by example, his dad helped him appreciate the natural world. He writes about his early love of drawing and shares his admiration of Jim Henson and Charles Schultz. Finally, he brings the story full circle by describing all the fun he had recently in the classroom. Each vignette enhances his understanding of his internal conflict and supports his desire to make a change in his career path.

Logan does a good job linking these experiences with his emotions. He finds meaning in his story by recognizing his strong desire to make a change. When he writes from the third-person perspective, he demonstrates understanding of his clients' needs. He knows he's good at what he does and can please his clients with the products he produces. He also understands he needs to be cautious about what he says to his clients and how he says it. If he's too open with his feelings, he could lose their business before he's ready to make a job shift.

Now Logan needs to figure out what to do about his conflict. He recognizes he has a negative attitude. Some of the words and phrases he's used support this conclusion. He says, "[I] hate myself for selling out to the establishment"; the job is "sucking the energy and life out of me," he "can't stand what I'm doing now," and it "makes me sick to my stomach." However, when he describes his dream job, the language is more positive. At one point, he uses the word "love" to describe drawing and reading, "fun" to describe his experience in the classroom, and "colorful, cartoonish" for his salsa packaging. His word choices match his feelings. There is honesty in his writing. He defines his dilemma and recognizes it needs to be resolved for his future happiness.

Let's see how he begins to tackle this stressful situation in his life.

Step Two: Affirm Your Stressless Future

Prompt One: Identify What Matters

> List three important values threatened by stress. Then insert each value into this sentence stem to test why it matters: What matters to me is __ because __ .

1. *Practicing my art*
2. *Doing work that doesn't harm the planet*
3. *Contributing financially to the day-to-day operation of the household*

What matters to me is practicing my art because art is who I am. Without it, I'll wither emotionally.

What matters to me is doing work that doesn't harm the planet because our world is precious. I don't want my art adding to the pollution of our oceans and forests!

What matters to me is contributing financially to the day-to-day operation of the household because my wife and I agreed early in our marriage that we would share equally in our living expenses. I also want my salary to be commensurate with my talents.

Prompt Two: Write Your Future Story, Your Vision

> Write your future story, linking your values to your vision of life with reduced stress.

My dream is to have a syndicated cartoon strip with an environmental message and a business with an educational focus. I'll work with chil-

dren, adults, anyone who'll listen, and teach them about conservation of our natural resources. Initially, I'll be a full-time employee with the county in their artist-in-residence program. This job will provide steady work and will help me build my resume until I can launch my new business, hire people who share my vision, and market our educational services across the U.S. This will make me happy!

Prompt Three: Write Your Affirmation

Create an "I" statement of what you want to do, be, or achieve in the future: I am . . .

I am a creative artist with a syndicated cartoon strip, running a business to educate children and adults about environmental issues.

Notes to Self: Reflection

The following three questions are a guide for your reflection. Respond to those that are relevant to you in this moment.

1. Describe how your affirmation confirms your values and your desired future.
2. As you described your future story, name any emotions that arose and how they influenced you.
3. Are you ready to be guided in Step Three to write your plan to make your future a reality? If yes, you're ready to go. If no, revisit your values, your future story, and your affirmation and modify as needed.

The values clarification step helped me visualize the future I want. I'm excited about drawing cartoons and educating children and adults. I'm a bit anxious about the challenge of redirecting my career. It won't be easy to move out of commercial art and still maintain my steady income. I know I can easily get sucked in to doing artwork I don't enjoy. After all, it pays the bills. As my job now stands, my core values don't align with it. I'm determined to find a way to practice art so that it doesn't harm the planet, and still earn a decent living, and share my talent in support of a cause bigger than myself.

I feel good about this new direction. My shoulders aren't as tight as they were when I started this writing exercise. I feel more energetic. I'm ready to move forward!

Commentary

Logan has a strong desire to leave commercial art and establish himself as a creative artist. He recognizes it will not be easy to make this career shift. Currently, he has a steady income and clients who appreciate his work. When Logan names his core values and writes about them, he notices they do not align with his present job. Values clarification, an important part of affirmative writing, helps him reflect on the core values that have a bearing on his career decisions and actions. With his new awareness, Logan recognizes his moral dilemma. Commercial art, as he is currently practicing it, is out of step with his values. He is now convinced he needs to renew his determination to make a career shift.

Affirmative writing supports behavior change. Logan's core values remind him he has a choice in determining his destiny. He can continue as he is, or he can make the shift to redesign his career. His strong affirmation—"I am a creative artist with a syndicated cartoon strip, running a business to educate children and adults about environmental issues"—gives him a goal and a way forward.

Step Three: Plan to Unravel Stress

Prompt One: Create Your Action Steps

> Write your affirmation from Step Two and create a list of the possible action steps you need for your affirmation to become a reality. Group like items, if any, and then assign a value of 1–5, with 5 being the highest priority.

Affirmation: I am a creative artist with a syndicated cartoon strip, running a business to educate children and adults about environmental issues.

Action items:

- *Create a portfolio featuring my cartoons and other creative art samples. (4)*
- *Find grants to support use of creative arts in education. (3)*
- *Explore artist-in-residence programs. (5) Start with the internet. School systems, museums, libraries, national parks, PBS, other organizations. Local, national, international opportunities. Application process? RFPs? Deadlines?*
- *Create a simple educational program I can take to farmers' markets, schools, and libraries as a road test. (1)*
- *See what's already out there for arts, environment, and sustainability. Maybe some new ideas will pop up. (3)*
- *Network, network, network. Who knows what leads I might develop if I start sharing my idea with other artists. Start with Linked In! (4)*
- *Develop a business plan. (4)*

Prompt Two: Action Script Your SMART Goals

For your priority action, define your SMART goal by responding to the following sentence stems. It's okay to specify more than one goal; simply repeat the process.

- **Specific:** *I will use the internet to find and research artist-in-residence programs that match my requirements.*
- **Measureable:** *I've achieved my goal when I come up with five solid programs I qualify for.*
- **Achievable:** *I will accomplish this by setting aside an hour after work until I find five programs I'm interested in. I'd love to find a good local one—perhaps with PBS.*
- **Realistic:** *I will do this now because I have the time to take on a job search and the need to make a career change.*
- **Time Bound:** *I will complete this within one month.*

Notes to Self: Reflection

The following questions are a guide for your reflection. Respond to those that are relevant to you in this moment.

1. As I reflect on my goals, I (notice, think, feel, am surprised by, etc.) . . .
2. What do you hope will be the outcome of completing your goals?

This is a good start. My SMART goal is specific and targeted. I think I can knock it out in less than a month, but I want to give myself enough time to do a good job. I need to keep my commercial art clients happy by doing the work they pay me for. I'm going to share this SMART goal with Lori. She's a bit tentative about my idea now, but as I share my SMART goals, I'll think she'll be on board 100%.

I've used SMART goals before when I wanted to finish a project on time. Goals motivate me—the more specific, the better. Remembering my past successes fuels my confidence. I know I can achieve this SMART goal and all the other goals I set for myself. I feel positive, enthusiastic, and ready to move forward!

Commentary

Logan prioritizes his goals and decides he will begin by exploring artist-in-residence programs. His first SMART goal is foundational to his plan to retool and refocus his career. Until he understands the market for creative artists and cartoonists, he won't know his direction. It is smart of him to begin by doing some research. Depending on what he finds, Logan can either move toward an artist-in-residence program or step back from it and come up with another plan. He'll write new SMART goals depending on what he discovers. That's the beauty of SMART goals. Logan uses them to direct his attention to what is relevant right now and to steer away from activities not related to his immediate goal. When you have a big project, it's easy to lose focus and get distracted. Logan wants his job search to be focused and managed. His SMART goals will improve his chances of successfully managing a career change.

Logan anticipates that each SMART goal he completes will probably give rise to goals he hasn't even thought of yet. In this way, one SMART goal will lead to another until he feels he's fully explored his options. Logan's challenge will be, to be patient with his exploration. His desire for a career shift represents a big change and a financial risk. If he doesn't manage his search process, it could lead to increased stress and disappointment.

Step Four: Reflect and Commit to Destress

Prompt One: Explore Your Readiness

> Write in response to one or more of these questions to assess your willingness, belief, and commitment to move forward.

1. Are you confident in your ability to move forward? If yes, move on. If not, what do you need to feel more confident?
2. On a scale of 1 to 5, with 5 being the most important, how important is it for you to enact your plan? If a 4 or 5, move on, and if less than 4 or 5, explore why.
3. What do you believe about yourself and your ability to do this? Write it down; then dig deeply to explore if this belief holds true. If not, change it to reflect your inner truth.
4. Describe your attitude toward making the changes you've identified in your action plan. For example, are you pumped and ready to go, fearful, or . . . ?
5. Describe how you will hold yourself accountable. How will you reward yourself?

There was a time in college when I lost all confidence in my artistic talent. I had a professor who didn't like my work. His criticism was harsh and I was devastated. I dropped out for a semester. Stopped drawing. Felt like a failure. Got a job waiting tables in one of the local diners. I was miserable, lost, and alone.

After a couple months of wallowing in self-pity, I just "woke up" one day. I missed my art and realized it was my lifeblood. I had to create; I had to draw. I picked up my colored pencils and sketched cartoons. They made me smile.

My dad's my role model. I remember how upset he'd get when there was a drought. He'd go out to the fields and watch the crops wither on the vine. He'd fret and fume, but then he'd bounce back. The next year, he'd start all over again with a new crop and new optimism. Farming is hard work and Dad was resilient. I learned about determination from him. He'd say, "Life has its ebb and flow. Don't give in to it when you're down!"

I think about my dad when I feel discouraged. He's my inspiration. Sure, I might be in a funk now, but I can dig my way out—nothing's as bad as losing your whole crop for lack of rain! I'll line up all my options before making my decision. I want to give myself time to complete a thoughtful search process. I'm ready to forge ahead by tackling one SMART goal at a time until I have my answer. It's important that I enact my plan. On a scale of 1–5, I'm definitely a 5!

Prompt Two: Reflect on Your Plan

Write a letter to a trusted person and describe the following:

- What you're going to do (action plan),
- What you've learned about yourself to make it happen,
- Why you're committed,
- Any obstacles that may arise,
- What you will do about them.

Logan decided to write a letter to his wife, Lori.

Dear Lori,

You've heard me talking, probably incessantly, about this crazy idea I have to shift out of commercial art to pursue my passion for teaching children and adults about the environment. I've realized that my core values do not align with my day-to-day work and it's making me crazy. It probably shows up in our relationship when I snap at you or retreat into myself. I'm sorry for that.

I want you to know I won't be reckless in making any career change decisions. We'll always talk first. I realize we have a lot to risk in terms of financial well-being and I don't want to create undue stress for myself or you. I have a good thing going now with commercial art. It pays the bills, but it's at the cost of my happiness.

Have you noticed that when I come home after working with children, I'm more energetic and relaxed than I am after a full day of commercial art? I hope it shows in my demeanor. The kids really respond well to my cartoons and my message. It's fun to see their excite-

ment when I teach them about respecting the earth. I'm passionate about taking this message to a larger audience.

I'm committed to doing my research first. I've decided to start by exploring artist-in-residence programs. If I can get one of those positions, it'll provide some job stability. I'm also going to do a lot of networking to see if there are other opportunities out there, and I'll redo my portfolio so it's up to date. I think these are good first steps. Will you support me in this first phase of exploration? I really want you to be as excited as I am about a possible career shift.

Prompt Three: Contract for Change

> Create a contract with yourself that positively states the key elements of your letter. Sign it, date it, and refer to it every day.

I, Logan, am committed to making a career shift, one step at a time. I will not shortchange the amount of time it takes to look at all the options. My happiness and my family's financial future are at stake.

When obstacles emerge, I'll read my affirmation, evaluate my SMART goals, and revise them as needed. I will also do the writing prompts from Step One of Write to Be Well to gain new insights into the obstacles I'm facing and the stress they're creating in my life.

Notes to Self: Reflection

> Reflect and write about what you are proudest of right now!

I know what I want and why. I have a plan and I'm committed to it. When obstacles arise, which I know they will, I'll make adjustments. I'm psyched! This is the beginning of a whole new chapter in my life. I'm ready to explore my opportunities!

Commentary

The contract for change is an important prompt in Write to Be Well. It's the writer's opportunity to digest and review all the thoughts, emotions, and questions that have arisen in his responses to the writing prompts. Logan's letter to his wife demonstrates that he understands his current situation and the risk he's assuming. He includes a statement of his plans and his pledge to include her in his decision-making process. His letter is an effective summary of all that he's learned about his stress and what he intends to do about it.

When Logan explores his confidence level, he recalls how his dad dealt with his stress. Writing about a role model often helps to clarify personal values. In Logan's case, his dad's fortitude serves as a reminder for Logan that he possesses the same strength and determination. In his commitment statement, Logan recognizes there will be obstacles to overcome. He has a plan and vows that the setbacks will not derail him. By writing about his feelings, plans, and commitment, Logan has a document to which he can refer, especially when he feels bogged down by life and confused by his direction.

Reflective writing is how Logan consolidates all his ideas into a few succinct statements. He understands the core of his stress and what's at stake in making a change. He's willing to take the risk, but on his own terms and in his own time. By setting clear boundaries, Logan will manage his life and his stress.

ROUND TWO OF WRITE TO BE WELL

Logan completed his first round of Write to Be Well over a two-week period. He picks up his pen again a week later to continue his journey in pursuit of his dream job. This time, he uses his own shortened version of Write to Be Well. He still follows the four-step process but does not go into all the detail he did before. Now he is writing to give himself feedback on the steps he's taken and to keep himself on task.

Before writing, he reminds himself of his commitment to "look at all the options" before making a career shift. His first SMART goal was to explore artist-in-residence programs.

Step One: Write Your Stress Story

I'm discouraged. There are tons of artist-in-residence programs, but most seem geared toward students who are still working on their degrees. And they don't pay much. I'm not even inspired to apply for a position. I'm disappointed with the results of my research.

Energy is at an all-time low. My anxiety about my career and lack of steady income are clouding my reason and balance. I want to let go of my frustration and define a new SMART goal. When I look at all I need to do in a day, I realize I have too much on my plate. There's volunteer work I really enjoy and job commitments I need to complete, but there just aren't enough hours in the day to do all of them and continue my job search. I have so integrated my professional work with my volunteering that it seems impossible to do the work I love and make a living at the same time. I need to figure out what I can let go of now so I can focus on what's important to me. Sometimes, I almost feel like giving up and getting a job at Walmart; at least it's honest work and it would provide a steady income!

Step Two: Affirm Your Stressless Future

My values haven't changed; neither has my goal to make a career shift. But to move forward, I need to relieve my stress by letting go of some of the stuff I'm doing now. When I do, it'll create more space in my day to resume my research. My affirmation stays the same: I am a creative artist with a syndicated cartoon strip, running a business to educate children and adults about environmental issues.

Step Three: Plan to Unravel Stress

My new SMART goal: Simplify my outside commitments so I have time to explore job opportunities, develop a business plan, network, look for grant money, and redesign my portfolio.

- **Specific:** *I will make a list of all the outside commitments I have on my plate. This includes the things I do at home as well as volunteer activities. Separate the list into two categories: (1) time-consuming, major commitments; (2) minor, easily completed commitments.*
- **Measureable:** *I've achieved my goal when I've dropped at least one activity from each of the two volunteer categories.*
- **Achievable:** *I will accomplish this by talking with each group to explain why I'm stepping back from my volunteer commitment.*

I've been involved with some of these groups for a long time, so it won't be easy. I don't like to disappoint people.

- **Realistic:** *I will do this now because I need to create more time in my schedule for all the work involved in a job search.*
- **Time Bound:** *I will give myself a month to accomplish this goal.*

Step Four: Reflect and Commit to Destress

I know this is what I need to do next, but not sure what I want to say to each group. I'll create another SMART goal with a strategy for letting go of these extra commitments. That should boost my confidence.

SMART Goal 2: Implement my strategic plan for letting go of outside commitments that limit the time I can devote to my job search.

- **Specific:** *I will write about the one major outside commitment I plan to drop. (1) Start with a reflection on what this activity has meant to me. Include how long I've been doing it, what I will miss about it, and what I won't miss. (2) Restate my values and explain how this activity does or does not reflect what's important to me. (3) Then write about who I will talk to and what I plan to say.*
- **Measureable:** *I've achieved my goal when I've written a minimum of three paragraphs.*
- **Achievable:** *I will accomplish this by expressing my thoughts on paper before making the call.*
- **Realistic:** *I will do this now because it's a critical step in clearing my calendar of extraneous activities. I like to write, so this feels like the right strategy for me.*
- **Timebound:** *I will complete this within the next 10 days.*

Commentary

Logan's use of Write to Be Well demonstrates the flexibility and scalability of the four-step process. The first time through, he wrote detailed answers to all the Write to Be Well prompts in each of the four steps. He took the time he needed to respond thoughtfully to every prompt. The second time through, he wrote brief answers to Steps One and Two, just enough to revisit his stress and reaffirm his goal. Then he spent the balance of his time writing two new SMART goals to address his realization that his first SMART goal to investigate artist-in-residence programs was not taking him in the direction he wanted. It took Logan less than thirty minutes to complete his writing, which resulted in a new direction, plus renewed energy and focus. His shortened version of Write to Be Well kept him on track and renewed his enthusiasm to reach his overarching goal, which is to create the space in his life to pursue new interests.

Like many of us who have setbacks, Logan became discouraged when his good intentions went awry. He started off enthusiastically and then began to fizzle out when he realized his first SMART goal was a dead end, but he wasn't ready to give up so easily! He used Write to Be Well a second time, resulting in the difficult decision to cut back on some of his activities. He then wrote two new SMART goals—one to sort through his commitments and a second to reduce the stress associated with his fear of disappointing his volunteer buddies. By revising his focus, Logan not only manages his stress but also moves closer to his overarching plan to realign his career with his core values.

Logan can use Write to Be Well in whatever way works best for him. Sometimes, he may want to write thoughtfully over a longer time. At other times, he may choose to go through the four steps in fifteen minutes or less by writing brief notes to himself. The key, as Logan knows, is to stay focused by revising, adjusting, and recommitting to his plan. As he says, "Write to Be Well provides the container I need for all my wild ideas. Writing helps me focus on a direction and makes my dream come alive. I'll keep writing until I reach my goal!"

8

SINGLE-PARENT JUGGLE

Amy, a single mother with three children, has been divorced for two years. It was a contentious separation, and the divorce continues along the same lines. Amy acknowledges that there are always two sides to every story, but deep down all she wants is for the aftermath of this divorce to settle into a respectful relationship of co-parenting. So far, this is not the case. Jason, her ex, sends her scathing emails and leaves phone messages accusing her of lying and being a bad mom. She says their relationship is toxic. They can't talk to each other without arguing.

So far, Jason has resisted Amy's repeated offers at mediation, preferring instead to have conflicts settled in court. She says, "If we weren't fighting all the time, I'd have over thirty thousand dollars extra in my bank account. But I need to stand up for my kids and what's best for them." Fortunately, Amy has a professional life as a corporate executive and can pay lawyers' fees, but she'd prefer to use this money to save for her children's college educations. As part of the divorce settlement, Jason has child support obligations until the children are eighteen. After that, they're on their own.

The ongoing conflict over what's best for the children is not only costing Amy a fortune, but it's driving her stress levels through the roof! She says, "The stress associated with our co-parenting affects every aspect of my life. I need to find a way to manage it because I know the stress isn't going away. I don't think Jason and I will ever agree on anything."

Amy likes to write. She often journals when she's traveling for business or when Jason has the kids, but she finds it's too hard to do when she's juggling work and kids full-time. She decided to test the flexibility and scalability of Write to Be Well by adapting the four steps to her busy lifestyle. She thought if she could write even a few sentences when she's feeling stressed, it might help her stay calm. She admits, "I can't change Jason. All I can do is manage my response to his tirades and the parenting issues he raises."

After familiarizing herself with the four-step Write to Be Well method, Amy decided to write briefly to some of the prompts in each step. She gave herself permission to ignore the principles of good grammar and sentence structure by writing phrases, partial sentences, or even one-word answers. She wanted Write to Be Well to work for her without putting additional pressure on her life, which was already too busy. Here's how she started out. From Amy's journal . . .

ROUND ONE OF WRITE TO BE WELL

Step One: Write Your Stress Story

Prompt Two: Write Your Own Story

> Write your story from the "I" perspective (first person), describing your thoughts and feelings surrounding the stressful situation, real or perceived.

Lack of co-parenting with Jason. I have tried everything with him—I've been kind and respectful, clever, taken the "high road," even tried to outsmart him when he's rude, inflexible. He doesn't want to co-parent in the best interest of our children. I don't understand why he fights and argues and casts blame on me all the time. He's so unreasonable— refuses mediation, although I'm willing. So off to court we go. I've won all four times.

His toxicity has crept into my life and no matter how much I try to keep up my shield, it's hurtful. I'm living on eggshells wondering when he'll hammer me on something again. I'm questioning who I am as a woman, an adult, and a mother.

All the stress of divorce and lack of positive co-parenting permeates every waking moment of my life. I feel so unsettled and my anxiety level is higher than it's ever been.

Notes to Self: Reflection

The following questions are a guide for your writing. Respond to those that are relevant to you in this moment.

1. What did you learn about yourself in responding to the prompts?
2. What did you notice about how stress plays out in your life? Did anything surprise you? Disappoint you? Annoy you? If so, be sure to name it!
3. What emotions did you uncover?
4. What happened in your body as you wrote? Did you experience any release of stress, or did you experience heightened anxiety?
5. Do you have clarity about the source of your stress, your thoughts, your feelings, and what they are "doing" to you? If not, you may want to go back and repeat the prompts.

I'm realizing just how unhappy this whole situation with Jason makes me—and I've been dealing with the stress of it for over two years! I want to address this problem, but I can't do it alone. That's what's so frustrating! I hoped Jason and I would co-parent like two reasonable adults—talk about parenting issues when little problems with the kids arose. But it's not possible. It's lonely being a single mom. Although this situation makes me feel sad, the writing's been cathartic. I have a clearer picture now about what's been heightening my stress.

Commentary

Step One asks you to write your stress story. You may say, "That's easy—it's my boss who's driving me crazy," or "It's my recent diagnosis of cancer that's scared me," or "It's my desire to stop smoking that's making me anxious." If you know, you can quickly name it and write about it. But if you're not sure about the source of your stress, you will benefit from writing to the same prompt multiple times, digging deeper into your feelings with each iteration until you "tell it" to your satisfaction. You decide how deep to go. Write to Be Well can be scaled up or down, depending on your needs.

Amy knows the source of her stress, so she chose to write about it only once. She easily names it as "co-parenting" and writes how her relationship with Jason escalates her stress levels. Naming the stress *and* linking the situation to your emotions is a minimal requirement for Step One of Write to Be Well. Amy doesn't have to write paragraphs about her stress, providing she connects the events to her emotions. As Pennebaker and his colleagues have demonstrated in their research, when thoughts and feelings are not expressed, it places people at risk for disease.[1] Spilling out your guts on paper reduces stress and sets you on a path to health and well-being. Remember, your writing is for your eyes only. Be honest, even if it's painful.

Amy completed Step One, Prompt Two, of Write to Be Well in less than fifteen minutes. She skipped the other prompts in Step One and went right to the heart of her story. She's ready to move on to Step Two, but she plans to return to Step One later as a way of monitoring and managing her responses to heightened stress.

Step Two: Affirm Your Stressless Future

Prompt One: Identify What Matters

> List three important values threatened by stress. Then insert each value into this sentence stem to test why it matters: What matters to me is __ because __ .

- *Connection—because it's the foundation of real relationships. Both parties are seen and heard.*
- *Authenticity—because it's important for me to be myself and allow others to be themselves. This creates the positive energy which resonates throughout my life and theirs.*
- *Respect for myself and others—because I believe in treating myself and others with integrity, experiencing the freedom to be myself.*

I am forever connected to Jason through our children. It will never be a meaningful relationship, but maybe I can find some peace if I stay true to my authentic self—a woman who is kind, compassionate, and honest.

Taking this position is respectful for me as well as Jason. Even if he doesn't give me a positive response, I'll feel better about who I am and how I represent myself in our communications.

As I read what I've written I realize it's up to me to reduce my stress; it will never come from anything Jason does or doesn't do. I have the power to shift my perspective.

Prompt Two: Write Your Future Story, Your Vision

Write your future story, linking your values to your vision of life with reduced stress.

Open, honest communication with Jason, free from the threat of litigation. A relationship based on a sincere desire to do what's best for our kids. Agreement to hire a parent coordinator for the tough conversations and decisions. Agreement that going to court is always the last, worst option.

In my future vision, I am less anxious and free to be myself, especially as a mother. My children notice my energy shift and this feels so much healthier. I have the energy to move forward, instead of constantly looking back at the coulda, woulda, shoulda of my life. I have a renewed sense of hope and peace. (Oh how I wish this were true!)

Prompt Three: Write Your Affirmation

Create an "I" statement of what you want to do, be, or achieve in the future: I am . . .

I am free to move forward with an unburdened heart. I feel healthy and vibrant now that I'm managing my personal stress.

Notes to Self: Reflection

The following three questions are a guide for your reflection. Respond to those that are relevant to you in this moment.

1. Describe how your affirmation confirms your values and your desired future.
2. As you described your future story, name any emotions that arose and how they influenced you.

3. Are you ready to be guided in Step Three to write your plan to make your future a reality? If yes, you're ready to go. If no, revisit your values, your future story, and your affirmation and modify as needed.

It feels good to name my values and recognize the fine qualities that define me. I see my challenge as one of staying true to myself in the face of Jason's anger and hostility.

   I'm not as confident about my future story. I don't think my relationship with Jason will ever be anything less than toxic. But I do think I can do a better job of controlling my anxiety by focusing on my core values. My hope for peace lies within myself.

Commentary

What matters? An honest response to this question informs Amy's thoughts, words, and actions in her relationship with Jason. What matters are her values. They are the foundation of her moral code, the heart of who she is underneath the day-to-day expression of her life. Incorporating her values into her life will help Amy make the decisions that will naturally lead her to a more fulfilling life experience. The answer to what matters is the most important prompt in Step Two.

Before Amy named her values, her life was out of balance. In her stressful relationship with her ex-husband, she forgot what was most important to her—connection, authenticity, and respect. Jason's anger rattled her and brought her down to where she lost her self-confidence in this relationship. Remembering her values renews her emotional strength so she can continue to discuss co-parenting issues with Jason. When she is true to herself, she is on firm ground. She may still feel the stress, but she will be able to manage it better, knowing her values are intact.

Amy's reflection in Step Two acknowledges that her future story of co-parenting with Jason may be unrealistic. Even so, she recognizes it is within her power to change the way she responds to Jason's vitriol. Her affirmation places the responsibility squarely on her shoulders and is a positive statement to guide her in managing future difficult situations. Step Two is one that Amy will return to whenever her stress escalates.

Her core values will bring her life back into balance by reminding her what matters.

Step Three: Plan to Unravel Stress

Initially, Amy said this plan-your-action step stumped her. She knew she couldn't control Jason's responses to her emails or phone calls. She said it wasn't until she went back to her affirmation that she recognized it was within her power to manage her stress levels by deciding how she responds to Jason.

Once again, Amy was pressed for time, so she decided merely to jot down her thoughts about moving forward. She could always come back to these prompts and write more later.

Prompt One: Create Your Action Steps

Write your affirmation from Step Two and create a list of the possible action steps you need for your affirmation to become a reality. Group like items, if any, and then assign a value of 1–5, with 5 being the highest priority.

I'd like to ignore Jason, but I can't do that when our children are involved. This is what I can do to manage my stress:

- *Restart my exercise regimen—find some new program that piques my interest and motivates me to exercise regularly (5)*
- *Read books in free time—to stimulate new interests and take mind off parenting concerns (3)*
- *Schedule short meditation daily—even a couple minutes of reflection helps to calm me (4)*
- *Schedule writing sessions daily—when I put my thoughts in writing, it's easier to work through my worries (4)*
- *Discover a working plan to ward off evening anxiety—that's a big one. Need to write about it to figure out how! (4)*
- *Don't respond to Jason's emails if I've had a glass of wine—wait until the next morning (5)*

Prompt Two: Action Script Your SMART Goals

> For your priority action, define your SMART goal by responding to the following sentence stems. It's okay to specify more than one goal; simply repeat the process.

I'm tackling the wine issue—it's the most effective way to help me right now. Doesn't take any preparation. It's decisive and immediately tangible!

- **Specific:** *I will refrain from answering emails from Jason if I've had a glass of wine! Better yet—I won't even read the email until the next morning.*
- **Measureable:** *I've achieved my goal when I wake up the next morning and then respond to his email.*
- **Achievable:** *I will accomplish this by distracting myself from all internet activities, including social media, and focusing instead on a book, a call to a friend, or some other pleasant activity.*
- **Realistic:** *I will do this now because Jason's emails often ruin my evening and put me in a bad mood. I get defensive and angry. Then I have trouble getting to sleep.*
- **Time Bound:** *I will complete this within two weeks and then evaluate my success.*

Notes to Self: Reflection

The following questions are a guide for your reflection. Respond to those that are relevant to you in this moment.

1. As I reflect on my goals, I (notice, think, feel, am surprised by, etc.) . . .
2. What do you hope will be the outcome of completing your goals?

I feel good about this SMART goal. It will be challenging, but I can do it. If one of Jason's emails comes in the evening, and I've had a glass of wine, I will just have to force myself not to look at it. Looking will be my downfall. If I read it, I'll start formulating a response in my head. That will take me down the proverbial rabbit hole by causing my stress to soar! Then I'll have a second glass of wine to help me sleep. This is not a healthy cycle. I think if I can follow this plan, I'll feel better about myself.

Commentary

Amy recognizes her challenge, but by writing a SMART goal, she improves her chances of success. She admits Jason's emails set her off, which releases adrenaline, cortisol, and other stress hormones to prepare her for "battle." Amy's heart starts to race, and then she reaches for another glass of wine to calm herself down. She does not want to head down this path.

As Locke and Latham's goal-setting theories prove, goals energize performance and motivate people to persist through time.[2] This is exactly what Amy needs to help her focus on herself and the behavior she wants to change. By writing down a SMART goal, she begins to understand what she can do to reduce her stress. Amy's SMART goal is her first step in taking charge of her stress and reframing her response to Jason. She can post her SMART goal all over the house if that's what she needs to keep her goal at the forefront of her mind.

Step Four: Reflect and Commit to Destress

Prompt One: Explore Your Readiness

> Write in response to one or more of these questions to assess your willingness, belief, and commitment to move forward.

1. Are you confident in your ability to move forward? If yes, move on. If not, what do you need to feel more confident?
2. On a scale of 1 to 5, with 5 being the most important, how important is it for you to enact your plan? If a 4 or 5, move on, and if less than 4 or 5, explore why.
3. What do you believe about yourself and your ability to do this? Write it down; then dig deeply to explore if this belief holds true. If not, change it to reflect your inner truth.
4. Describe your attitude toward making the changes you've identified in your action plan. For example, are you pumped and ready to go, fearful, or . . . ?

5. Describe how you will hold yourself accountable. How will you reward yourself?

I'm ready to change my behavior to save my integrity. I've done it before and I can do it again. Bob was my boyfriend in college. That was a disastrous relationship! He pressured me to be sexually active with him when I wasn't ready. But like all college kids, I was drinking and smoking pot, which reduced my resistance and got me into trouble. I got out of that relationship with the help of a few good friends who were willing to listen and support me. Thankfully the whole incidence was merely a blip in my college career. But it was a relationship lesson. I learned it was within my power to change my behavior and correct the course of my actions.

Prompt Two: Reflect on Your Plan

Write a letter to a trusted person and describe the following:

- What you're going to do (action plan),
- What you've learned about yourself to make it happen,
- Why you're committed,
- Any obstacles that may arise,
- What you will do about them.

Dear Me,

I'm already doing what I need to do to protect my children, but it's been at a high cost to me. Jason pushes all my buttons. I know it's totally within my control to change the way I react to him, but it's hard to control my rage when he is so unreasonable. I'm making a commitment to myself to be present in this relationship in a different way. I want to be authentic and respectful. My first line of attack: I will not read or respond to his emails if I've had a glass of wine. It lowers my defenses and makes me more vulnerable to his hateful words. By taking even this small step, I can move forward with an unburdened heart, knowing that I'm being true to myself, my values, and my beliefs. I feel empowered by making this commitment.

Prompt Three: Contract for Change

> Create a contract with yourself that positively states the key elements of your letter. Sign it, date it, and refer to it every day.

I, Amy, agree to stay true to my core values. I place connection, authenticity, and respect at the forefront of my life, knowing that when I am true to my values, I am happier and more at peace with myself. When obstacles arise, I will talk with my counselor and dear friends who believe in me.

Notes to Self: Reflection

> Reflect and write about what you are proudest of right now!

This last step helps me solidify my commitment to change. I know I'm a strong woman who's fiercely protective of my children. When Jason is unreasonable, I promise myself I will thoughtfully consider my response before emailing or calling him. When he refuses to listen to my side, I will stop the conversation before it deteriorates into a yelling match. This is one way to honor and respect myself. The other is to be fully aware of how wine lowers my defenses, increases my stress if I'm in a confrontation, and escalates the argument. I cannot be strong for my children if I've had a glass of wine. If there is no emergency, I will not answer emails in the moment!

I'm probably repeating myself, but it helps me to write what I will and won't do again. I'm pleased with the initial outcome of my Write to Be Well plan. I know this is only the beginning, but it's a good first step.

Commentary

Reflective writing is the summation of what you've learned about yourself and what you'll commit to doing to make the lifestyle changes you desire. This is not an easy step. As Amy discovered, it's hard to accept our role in a relationship that's gone bad, especially when there is little hope of repairing it. In her final entries, Amy understands the limitations of her connection with Jason and outlines an initial plan to change her response to his emails. She is honest and realistic about what she can do, freely acknowledging that when she has wine, she is an ineffective communicator.

When we write reflectively, we become our own counselor. We look at what we've said, comment on what we've learned, and make a conscious decision either to change or not to change. This final step in Write to Be Well is an opportunity to transform our old ways into new ways of acting and being. Writing gives us the power to step outside of ourselves and view our actions from another perspective. Sometimes we discover new things about our behavior, which will aid us in managing stress and living a healthier, happier lifestyle.

Amy is well on her way to testing out some new behaviors. Even if she discovers she's taken on more than she can handle, she's allowed herself to consult with a counselor and share her burdens with a few trusted friends. Her challenge now, as she implements her plan, is to keep going, even when she has setbacks. As she discovers, the four steps in Write to Be Well can be worked and reworked again and again. Let's see how she proceeds.

ROUND TWO OF WRITE TO BE WELL

Amy knows the Write to Be Well steps and now uses the process, without all the prompts, to help herself accomplish her first SMART goal: "I will not open, read, or respond to one of Jason's emails if I've had a glass of wine."

Step One: Write Your Stress Story

Here we go again! It's Friday night. The kids are with Jason and there's an email in my inbox. It's 9 pm. I've had a glass of wine and I refuse to open this email now. I just hope I can sleep tonight without worrying about what he might have said. When I left the kids at 5 pm, everything was fine. If there was an emergency, he'd call. I'll read my book instead and address this in the morning. Breathe!

Step Two: Affirm Your Stressless Future

I want to be true to myself, manage stress, and be an excellent mom. Can I do all three in the context of this relationship? I'm going to try.

Step Three: Plan to Unravel Stress

I promised myself I wouldn't answer emails if I'd had a glass of wine. Instead, I'm going to

- *call my best friend and ask for her support*
- *do one of my yoga tapes*
- *read my book*
- *go to bed*

Step Four: Reflect and Commit to Destress

My action steps will help me relax and focus on something other than that email. I'm ready to give it a try.

Commentary

In only five minutes, Amy jotted down how she was feeling, reminded herself of her SMART goal, and planned a few action steps to help her stay on track. She reaffirmed her commitment to try out this new behavior and then got started by dialing a friend who knows her story.

The simple act of writing down her action plan and reaffirming her commitment kept Amy from ruminating about what to do when the email popped up. She highlighted how she was feeling and formulated another plan.

Let's see how she did when she practiced Write to Be Well on the following day.

ROUND THREE OF WRITE TO BE WELL

Notes to Self: Reflection

I made it! I waited until this morning to read the email. I was a bit restless when I went to bed, but slept well once I got to sleep. Jason wanted to know if I would pick up the kids the next day as he had something to do. Of course I said yes even though it's an hour's drive each way. I do wish he'd stay on plan. I'm beginning to see that I do more than my fair share of delivering and picking up, which means I'm letting him off the hook! I just need to remember that I'm doing it for the children. I don't want them to think they're an inconvenience.

It's time to write another SMART goal. I'm feeling anxious again.

Step Three: Plan to Unravel Stress

Prompt Two: Action Script Your SMART Goals

I need a plan to address my anxiety. I'd like to get back into exercising on a regular basis, especially when I feel anxious. I haven't had an exercise regimen since I broke my foot six months ago. I know I will feel better if I can just get started.

- **Specific:** *I will find a personal trainer who is a Pilates instructor. I've never tried Pilates, yet I understand it's good for building up the core muscles.*
- **Measureable:** *I've achieved my goal when I've located a Pilates instructor. I'll search the internet, do a few follow-up phone calls, and check in with a friend who takes Pilates.*
- **Achievable:** *I've achieved my goal when I've located a Pilates instructor.*
- **Realistic:** *I will do this now because I need to reduce my stress and anxiety. Exercise helps me.*
- **Time Bound:** *Yes, two weeks to find an instructor and get going.*

Notes to Self: Reflection

I'm ready! I've always wanted to try Pilates. Since this program is new to me, it should keep me motivated and help me manage my anxiety and stress. When I looked back at my action plan, I noticed that exercise was one of my top priorities. I like Pilates's focus on core strength. When I feel strong, I'm more confident. I need an extra dose of confidence right now to deal with Jason and maintain my integrity. I'm confident I can find a trainer and get started.

Commentary

In round three, Amy begins her writing session by reflecting on her previous night's success in not answering Jason's email. Although she feels good about that incident, her reflection uncovers a new stress. She realizes Jason often takes advantage of her willingness to drive their children between houses. She decides it's time to tackle another SMART goal, one that will address her anxiety when Jason pushes the boundaries of their relationship. She will continue to use her first SMART goal when she needs to respond to an email, and she will design a new SMART goal to address her anxiety. Now she is working on two SMART goals.

This is how Amy will progress toward her goal to reduce her stress. Each SMART goal represents a step in the right direction and is tied into her action plan. She will find that as she implements each SMART goal, she builds resilience and begins to reshape her story to reflect a woman who maintains her values even through difficult, challenging situations. Her new habit will provide greater consistency in her relationship with Jason. Although she may still get rattled at times, her writing will bring her back to herself and the life she wants to create for herself and her children.

ROUND FOUR OF WRITE TO BE WELL

Amy knows the Write to Be Well method and feels comfortable with the four steps. She finds the process helpful and often turns to it when she's feeling stressed and needs a quick plan to address it. She uses it in her relationship with Jason as well as other situations that pop up at work. Here's her "quick and dirty" version, which she writes on a scrap of paper no bigger than a napkin!

Stress: Help! My boss moved our project deadline up by two weeks.

Affirmation: I am authentic and respectful in all relationships.
SMART goal:

- *Specific: Ask for additional resources to get the job done on time.*
- *Measureable: I've identified two additional people to help put financial picture together.*
- *Achievable: Tap into my network of subcontractors*
- *Realistic: Depends on budget, but I think I can find the money.*
- *Timebound: Set up appointment with boss today and get process started!*

Notes to Self: Stay true to self and what I need. Be respectful in asking. Negotiate if necessary.

Commentary

Amy knows exactly what's causing her stress. She jots it down. The words she chooses to describe her stress make the stress real and tangible. Then she affirms herself just as she has done before in her relationship with Jason. Writing her affirmation reminds her of what she values. In Step Three, she briefly outlines her SMART goal. This is what she needs to do to be authentic when asking her boss for what she needs. She sets a time limit, knowing she must act quickly. Her reflection verifies that this action is appropriate as a first step. Other SMART goals will follow as she works her way toward her new deadline.

It took Amy less than five minutes to get on top of this stressful situation. The act of writing stopped her from ruminating about her stress and helped her focus on what she needs to do. In Write to Be Well, each step builds on the next to create an integrated writing method. The writing is scalable and flexible, which means that once you understand the four steps, you can write to all the prompts or hone in on what is essential in the moment. You can write as much as you want or as little.

It's the process of writing that makes the difference in stress management. As explained in chapter 2, writing is effective because you can disclose your emotions privately and without the judgment of others. The words you choose reflect your feelings. You can easily gauge how positive or negative you're feeling by noticing your choice of words.

Finally, writing helps you find meaning in stressful events. When you understand what's going on in your life, you grow and learn from your experiences.

9

TOO SWEET TO HANDLE—MANAGING DIABETES

Yvonne knew it was just a matter of time before she would be diagnosed with diabetes. Her family's genetic predisposition to the disease, plus a long history of being overweight, made her a perfect target. Her father along with aunts, uncles, and cousins on her dad's side of the family had all lived and struggled with the disease. As she left the doctor's office, all she could think about was her dad, who was diagnosed with type 2 diabetes at her same age of thirty-two. He faced complication after complication. First, it was neuropathy, nerve damage causing a tingling and numbness in his feet. Then his eyesight began to fail. Finally, it was a heart attack that killed him when he was only fifty-nine years old. Yvonne wondered if this would be her fate too. She left the doctor's office feeling numb and overwhelmed.

The doctor explained that diabetes is a complex condition brought on by obesity, a sedentary lifestyle, and/or genetics. He also informed her that if she managed her diabetes, she might be able to reverse her symptoms. He encouraged her to lose thirty pounds and to exercise daily. "Easy for you to say," she thought. "I've been trying to lose these same thirty pounds for the last fifteen years."

As she left the doctor's office, Yvonne ticked off the number of diets she'd tried and the exercise classes she'd started and dropped out of. It was painful to remember all her failed attempts. This time she knew she'd have to try harder. She didn't want diabetes to shorten her life as it had her father's. She decided to reach out for help by consulting with a diabetes educator and nutritionist and joining a support group. She wanted to walk this path with other people struggling with the same disease.

Yvonne joined the diabetes support group at her local hospital and learned about an upcoming workshop on the Write to Be Well method. Since she'd dabbled in journal writing off and on throughout her life, she decided to give it a try, hoping that writing would keep her focused and on a healthy track. She aspired to a lifestyle change, not just a short-term diet and exercise routine. To keep herself engaged for the long term, she knew she needed a program to help her set goals, be accountable, and renew her commitment when obstacles arose. She found her answer in Write to Be Well.

Yvonne has been using Write to Be Well for a year. In the following journal excerpts, she shares pages out of her journal to illustrate how she's managed the ups and downs of diabetes. In her first entries, you'll see how she responded to her initial diagnosis. Then we'll drop in on her journal writings periodically over the next few months, so you can follow her progress as she handles the challenges posed by living with a chronic disease. From Yvonne's journal . . .

ROUND ONE OF WRITE TO BE WELL

August: initial diagnosis.

Step One: Write Your Stress Story

Prompt One: Complete This Sentence Stem

The stressful situation (real or perceived) I am facing is *an overwhelming sense of shock and dismay at my recent diagnosis of type 2 diabetes.*

Prompt Two: Write Your Own Story

> Write your story from the "I" perspective (first person), describing your thoughts and feelings surrounding the stressful situation, real or perceived.

I'm scared. Complications from diabetes killed Dad. Now I'm looking at the same outcome. I'm afraid for myself and for what lies ahead. I need to make big lifestyle changes, but I don't know where to begin. The doctor's given me pamphlets to read, dietary suggestions to help me lose weight, and prescriptions to see a CDE [certified diabetes educator] *and nutritionist. He wants me to lose 30 pounds, bring down my A1C* [a blood test that measures your average blood sugar during the previous two to three months] *from its current level of 7.5 to normal levels of 6.0 or less and without medication. He says there's a good chance the disease will go into remission if I lose the extra weight.*

I dread the thought of dieting and exercising. I've struggled with both since I was a kid. I remember how I used to avoid doing laps around the field in gym class by faking a sprained ankle. I doubt that the instructor believed me, but I got away with it. The doctor said I should build up to 150 minutes of exercise a week. That's impossible! I don't have time for this—I'm starting from 0 exercise!

It's hard to change old habits. I'm stressed thinking about giving up my comfort foods. No more mint chocolate chip ice cream, blueberry muffins, fried chicken with mashed potatoes, or soft drinks. Instead I'll be eating dry chicken breasts, broccoli, and fruit. I'll be sticking my fingers with needles to test blood sugar levels and recording everything I eat and every step I take. I feel like there's a gremlin sitting on my shoulder, taunting me, laughing, saying things like, "I told you this would happen if you didn't change your ways!"

Prompt Three: Shift Your Perspective

Now write your story from another person's point of view (third person).

Dad. What would you say? He'd probably be sympathetic, but firm. He'd give me advice, like: "Yvonne, you can do this. Don't end up like me. Learn from my mistakes. Diabetes is a tough, unrelenting disease, but you can manage it. Follow the doctor's advice and seek the help you need. Make diabetes a priority in your life. It's that important!"

My sister would remind me to stay positive. She'd say I was being overly dramatic and negative about this diagnosis. She'd challenge me to think of other times I'd faced and overcome a problem. She'd say, "Remember when you went to Liberia on a humanitarian mission? No one would go with you, but you were determined. You booked a flight, hopped on that plane all by yourself, and traveled hundreds of miles to teach children how to read. I know that wasn't easy, but you found your way, and came home a new person—filled with self-confidence! Think about other times you've confronted challenges and been just as success-ful. You're not a loser!"

Then she'd say, "Yvonne, I've never known you to back away from a difficult task. The doctor's already given you a goal—lose 30 pounds and exercise 150 minutes a week. Break it down into small steps and then begin. Don't expect overnight success. You can beat the negative consequences of diabetes but you've got to make the effort. Yvonne, I'm counting on you to rally." Then she'd tell me to call her when I feel discouraged—any time, day or night!

Notes to Self: Reflection

The following questions are a guide for your writing. Respond to those that are relevant to you in this moment.

1. What did you learn about yourself in responding to the prompts?
2. What did you notice about how stress plays out in your life? Did anything surprise you? Disappoint you? Annoy you? If so, be sure to name it!
3. What emotions did you uncover?
4. What happened in your body as you wrote? Did you experience any release of stress, or did you experience heightened anxiety?
5. Do you have clarity about the source of your stress, your thoughts, your feelings, and what they are "doing" to you? If not, you may want to go back and repeat the prompts.

This is not going to be easy, but I can hear my father's and my sister's voices telling me to buck up and forge ahead. I want to feel motivated, but I'm not quite there. I'm still wallowing in self-pity. I have strong memories of backsliding every time I've tried a new diet or joined a new exercise program. I can feel the stress in my body. My stomach's a knot. I'm having trouble breathing. My writing hasn't released any anxiety. I feel more stressed and anxious than ever before. I'm just not sure I can manage diabetes with diet and exercise. Isn't there a pill I can take?

Commentary

Yvonne's writing reflects her discouragement. She focuses on her diagnosis and the challenges that lie ahead. She hasn't been able to picture a future that's better for herself than what her father experienced. Her writing reflects her distress. Although her father's and sister's encouraging voices are in her head, they are not strong enough to overcome her negative feelings about her diagnosis. She is still grieving for her life before diabetes.

Yvonne decides to do Step One again. She elects to dig deeper to uncover more of her story and emotions before moving on to Step Two.

Step One: Write Your Stress Story (Again!)

Prompt One: Complete This Sentence Stem

The stressful situation I'm facing is *a history of failed dieting and exercising.*

Prompt Two: Write Your Own Story

It's the extra 30 pounds I'm carrying that's the source of my stress. I have so many bad memories linked to a lifetime of being overweight. I wouldn't call myself obese, but I've always been "plump." I was a skinny kid until I was ten. When I went through puberty, I gained weight and my bad snacking habits added pounds I couldn't shed. Besides, who diets at that young age? By the time I was sixteen, I was already yo-yoing! I'd go on a starvation diet to get into a prom dress, lose a few pounds, and then gain it right back. A few of the mean girls taunted me and called me "fatty." I was embarrassed about my body. Gym class and showers in the girls' locker room were torture. I felt their eyes staring at my rolls of fat. It was horrible!

In college, I started some serious dieting. I tried every new diet on the market—Atkins, South Beach, Paleo, Ketogenic, Weight Watchers—and none of them worked for me. Of course, I couldn't maintain the program. I'd be in the middle of a term paper or facing finals and I'd lose my focus. Start snacking! Give up! Tell myself I was too stressed to diet. This pattern has repeated itself in my working life.

I won't even go into the exercise piece now, but it's just as bad. Start—stop—fail! That seems to be my mantra. I just don't know how I can go through this cycle one more time.

Prompt Three: Shift Your Perspective

What would my best friend, Lucy, say? She'd get on my case. Tell me to stop whining. She'd say, "Yvonne, this is your life you're playing with! Do not end up like your father! You can lose the weight. Remember, you don't have to lose 30 pounds in a week. This is a lifestyle change you need to make. Think about it as a gradual shift in a pattern you've developed since you were a kid. It's not easy to turn those old habits around. But I know you can do it. I'll hang in there with you. We can share healthy recipes and exercise together. You like to dance. Let's take a Zumba class together. It'll be fun."

Notes to Self: Reflection

I think I've been more honest this second time around. It's my history of dieting and all those memories that's really stressing me out! I'm afraid of failing again but I realize that this time, it's up to me to save my life. I can't fail! I don't want to.

The knot in the center of my stomach is starting to go away. I'm surprised that getting these memories and emotions down on paper has released some of my stress.

I'm lucky to have a good friend like Lucy. I know she'll support me however she can. She'll be honest—tell me when I'm being too hard on myself or when I'm whining. She's a good kick in the butt type of friend! I'll set up a coffee date with her and share what I'm facing.

Commentary

It took Yvonne two rounds of Step One writing to identify the core of her stress. She leaves this step now with a clear understanding of what she's facing. She realizes the diabetes diagnosis awakened a stress about her body that has roots in her childhood. It's an old stress that she's tried to bury, but like so many of us, the old stories tend to reappear at critical times in our lives, forcing us to deal with them until they're resolved. Yvonne knows she must confront the demons of the past before she can chart her path to wellness.

Step Two: Affirm Your Stressless Future

Prompt One: Identify What Matters

> List three important values threatened by stress. Then insert each value into this sentence stem to test why it matters: What matters to me is __ because __ .

1. *Faith*
2. *Friendship*
3. *Honesty*

What matters to me is my faith because I believe God wants me to live up to my full potential. This includes taking care of myself so I can grow into the person I'm meant to be.

What matters to me is friendship because I love being with people and getting to know them. I'm an extrovert. I treasure the friends in my life and want to widen my circle.

What matters to me is honesty because I tell people what I think and want them to be just as honest with me.

Prompt Two: Write Your Future Story, Your Vision

> Write your future story, linking your values to your vision of life with reduced stress.

I'm 30 pounds slimmer. Yeah me! I'm more energetic than I've ever been before. I'm choosing healthy alternatives for snacks and meals. Occasionally, I splurge on a small treat, like a cookie. Most of the time, I'm happy with my food choices. Vegetables taste good now that I've given up sugar. I'm dancing three times a week and loving it! Twice a week, I go to a Zumba class with Lucy. Once a week I take a ballroom dancing lesson, and when I can I attend the dances. It's so much fun!

It's taken me three years to make my lifestyle change. I lost the weight slowly, but I've kept it off. I know the exercise helps a lot. I love my new wardrobe too, especially my dance outfits!

My values help me stay focused and on target with my goals. My faith provides a firm foundation for change. I'm following my belief that God wants what's best for me and is with me every step of the way. I pray for guidance and strength when I get discouraged. My healthy lifestyle has introduced me to a great group of new friends who also practice healthy habits. The diabetes support group reminds me that I'm not alone. I'm being brutally honest with myself. When I cheat on my diet, I acknowledge it, forgive myself, and then let it go. It's a good practice that helps me pick myself up when I've stumbled along this path.

I'm smiling more! Life is good and my diabetes is under control, without medication.

Prompt Three: Write Your Affirmation

Create an "I" statement of what you want to do, be, or achieve in the future: I am . . .

I am a healthy woman, living a vibrant, stress-free life and successfully managing my diabetes.

Notes to Self: Reflection

The following three questions are a guide for your reflection. Respond to those that are relevant to you in this moment.

1. Describe how your affirmation confirms your values and your desired future.
2. As you described your future story, name any emotions that arose and how they influenced you.
3. Are you ready to be guided in Step Three to write your plan to make your future a reality? If yes, you're ready to go. If no, revisit your values, your future story, and your affirmation and modify as needed.

I loved writing my future story and affirmation. I envisioned myself living a healthy life. Diet and exercise weren't a drag! I see it now as a matter of perspective. I can grumble and complain about every healthy bite I take or I can make it into a game of sorts and find some new friends who will share my eating and exercising adventures. It's up to me! I know if I grumble, my stress will skyrocket!

Naming three values was also an important step. Faith bolsters my courage, and friends, especially those in my diabetes group, will support me along the way. I'll be honest with them and encourage them to be honest with me. I hope we'll reach out to each other when we're feeling discouraged. I know talking about my feelings with a friend has always helped me. I want to be that friend to others too. I also want to stop lying to myself—these extra 30 pounds do matter. I'm optimistic about the future and excited to set some goals. I'm ready to begin again.

Commentary

Yvonne concludes this step with a positive attitude and a clear vision of the future she desires. Her writing is punctuated with positive language. She talks about feeling energetic, happy with food choices, enjoying dancing, being motivated by her values, finding supportive friends, and being optimistic. She even states, "I'm smiling more!" Yvonne no longer sounds like the person from Step One who was stressed about diabetes ending her life prematurely.

At the core of Step Two is the statement of values. Yvonne picks three that matter most to her—faith, friendship, and honesty. Writing them down and explaining why they are important to her activates her brain and creates new neural pathways she can access whenever she feels discouraged. Her values build ego strength and will motivate her when the going gets tough. The act of writing will help her remember why her healthy lifestyle is critical to her future well-being. The affirmation gives her a goal, which she can now turn into a concrete plan with steps.

Step Three: Plan to Unravel Stress

Prompt One: Create Your Action Steps

> Write your affirmation from Step Two and create a list of the possible action steps you need for your affirmation to become a reality. Group like items, if any, and then assign a value of 1–5, with 5 being the highest priority.

Affirmation: I am a healthy woman, living a vibrant, stress-free life and successfully managing my diabetes.
Action items:

1. *Monitor blood sugar with finger sticks four times a day (5)*
2. *Join a Zumba class with Lucy and attend regularly twice a week (3)*
3. *Take the stairs at work rather than the elevator (3)*
4. *Meet with a nutritionist to discuss dietary needs, healthy snacks, how to create balanced meals, and portion control (4)*
5. *Join a diabetes support group led by a CDE (5)*
6. *Create a personal accountability chart to track my weight loss and monitor exercise (3)*
7. *Post my values on the bathroom mirror to remind myself why I am doing this! (2)*
8. *Pray for guidance every morning (3)*
9. *Get to bed by 11 pm 5 days a week (3)*
10. *Write a short journal entry daily using Write to Be Well to keep me accountable to my goals (4)*

Focusing on diabetes education is probably the most important thing I can do now. The more I know about the disease and the way it affects me, the less stressed I'll be. I want to understand the relationship between stress and blood sugar, and how exercise and diet are critical in managing the disease. So I'm starting with two action steps, all rolled into one SMART goal.

Prompt Two: Action Script Your SMART Goals

For your priority action, define your SMART goal by responding to the following sentence stems. It's okay to specify more than one goal; simply repeat the process.

- **Specific:** *I will monitor and chart blood sugar, stress, and emotions, find and join a CDE-led support group.*
- **Measurable:** *I've achieved my goal when I've collected, monitored, and charted blood sugar daily for a month and joined a support group.*

- *Achievable:* I will accomplish this by filling in the chart the doctor gave me and joining the support group at the hospital the doctor recommended.
- *Realistic:* I will do this now because I need a baseline of understanding about diabetes and how it affects my body.
- *Timebound:* I will complete this within one month.

Notes to Self: Reflection

The following questions are a guide for your reflection. Respond to those that are relevant to you in this moment.

1. As I reflect on my goals, I (notice, think, feel, am surprised by, etc.) . . .
2. What do you hope will be the outcome of completing your goals?

Although my first goal isn't exciting, it will be challenging. Somehow, I need to remember to monitor my blood sugar until it becomes a habit. My new routine will be one finger stick before each meal and then again at bedtime.

I'm looking forward to joining the diabetes support group. I'm usually more successful meeting a challenge when I'm part of a team than if I go it alone. Group members will be my cheering squad. We'll motivate each other and I'll learn the ins and outs of diabetes from the CDE and the other participants. Diabetes can be managed, but first I need to understand the disease and how my body responds to high and low sugar levels.

Commentary

Yvonne is off to a good start. She knows what she needs to do to understand diabetes self-care, and this knowledge will ease her stress. She'll monitor her blood sugar and focus on education before she launches her diet and exercise programs. This makes sense. Diabetes is a complex disease with many variables. She is laying the foundation for a lifestyle change.

Yvonne's word choice reflects her commitment to action. She uses strong verbs, like *monitor, chart, join, attend, motivate.* Each verb speaks to her desire to get moving, to do something, to make changes! Her SMART goal sets the stage for the work that lies ahead.

Step Four: Reflect and Commit to Destress

Prompt One: Explore Your Readiness

> Write in response to one or more of these questions to assess your willingness, belief, and commitment to move forward.

1. Are you confident in your ability to move forward? If yes, move on. If not, what do you need to feel more confident?
2. On a scale of 1 to 5, with 5 being the most important, how important is it for you to enact your plan? If a 4 or 5, move on, and if less than 4 or 5, explore why.
3. What do you believe about yourself and your ability to do this? Write it down; then dig deeply to explore if this belief holds true. If not, change it to reflect your inner truth.
4. Describe your attitude toward making the changes you've identified in your action plan. For example, are you pumped and ready to go, fearful, or . . . ?
5. Describe how you will hold yourself accountable. How will you reward yourself?

I'm confident I can achieve my first SMART goal. After that, I'm not so sure. I think I'm just going to have to tackle this huge lifestyle change one step at a time. I'll gain more self-confidence along the way. I have a lot to deal with to become the woman of my affirmation. I believe I have the ability and certainly the desire to become her, but this is not a quick fix!

I believe my first SMART goal is appropriate for where I am as a newly diagnosed person with diabetes. I'm feeling stressed and overwhelmed, knowing there are so many health issues to address. I want to be patient with myself, yet move steadily forward. I will hold myself accountable by playing mind games, like charting my progress and setting up a reward system. I already know that when I lose 10 pounds I'm going to treat myself to some new exercise clothes!

Prompt Two: Reflect on Your Plan

Write a letter to a trusted person and describe the following:

- What you're going to do (action plan),
- What you've learned about yourself to make it happen,
- Why you're committed,
- Any obstacles that may arise,
- What you will do about them.

Dear Lucy,

You're it! My one good friend who's already told me she'd support me throughout this lifestyle change. It's a huge one, so I hope you're prepared for a long ride! Here's what I've decided. I'm going to build a strong foundation for change by learning as much as I can about diabetes. This disease has impaired the lives of so many of my family members. It'll be a huge challenge and maybe I can even bring some of my relatives along on this journey to wellness. Wouldn't that be great!!

My first goal is to monitor and chart my blood sugar, stress, and emotions. I need to understand how diabetes affects me and what happens to my sugar levels when I'm feeling stressed. I'll also join a support group led by a CDE. This way, I'll get the straight scoop on how to manage diabetes. There's a lot to learn and I don't want to be misinformed. The CDE will be my subject-matter expert.

Lucy, I'm giving you permission to nudge me if you see me slipping back into old habits. I know diabetes is serious and I'm committed to a healthy lifestyle that supports stable blood sugar levels and low stress. I'm pumped up and ready to get started!

Prompt Three: Contract for Change

Create a contract with yourself that positively states the key elements of your letter. Sign it, date it, and refer to it every day.

Recognizing that this is just the first step in a long-range plan, I, Yvonne, promise to monitor blood sugar, emotion, and stress. My initial action plan will be to:

1. *chart blood sugar levels four times a day*

2. *at the same time, I'll rate my daily stress level from 1 (low) to 5 (high) and*
3. *note my emotions so I can correlate blood glucose, stress, and emotion*
4. *join a diabetes support group*

Signed, sealed, and delivered! Yvonne

Notes to Self: Reflection

Reflect and write about what you are proudest of right now!

I know what I need to do for my first step. I'm proud of myself for using the Write to Be Well method. It's taken some time and thought, but I'm in a better place now than when I started. Writing SMART goals will be very helpful as I pursue my long-term plan to lose 30 pounds and lead a healthy life. I especially like the fact that SMART goals are specific, action oriented, and time bound. I have a long road ahead of me, but I know exactly how to get started. This is all good!

Commentary

Yvonne has completed all four steps of Write to Be Well. She's told her story, affirmed a future of health and well-being, created a plan, and committed to change. The transformation that takes shape in the days and months ahead will be entirely up to her. She has the tools to make it happen, but she needs the resolve to stick to her goals until she's formed new health habits.

In this last step of Write to Be Well, Yvonne reflects honestly on the journey ahead. She explores her readiness to change, acknowledging that she can only commit to one step at a time. She's realistic in viewing diabetes as a lifestyle disease—change doesn't happen overnight. In her letter, she enlists Lucy to support her through the ups and downs of whatever lies ahead. She professes to be excited to begin and knows exactly what to do to get started.

Her reflective writing suggests she has grown in self-knowledge. She understands the devastating impact of diabetes on her health and has created a new vision for herself, one of health and vibrancy. Her writing is positive and upbeat, much different from her first journal entry, and an indication that she is ready to undertake this challenge.

In the journal entries that lie ahead, you'll see how Yvonne confronts the issues that arise since she was diagnosed in August to her last entry a year later. You'll also note that she consistently follows the four-step Write to Be Well method but has shortened her answers depending on how much time she has in her day.

ROUND TWO OF WRITE TO BE WELL

November: three months after diagnosis.

Step One: Write Your Stress Story

I'm dreading the holidays. Don't know if I can maintain my new healthy lifestyle? I've lost eight pounds by giving up most sweets and joining a Zumba class with Lucy. I'm feeling positive. I've learned a lot about diabetes, especially how my blood sugar rises dramatically when I'm feeling stressed. I'm afraid holidays will undo all the progress I've made. It'll be hard not to nibble on treats and my Zumba class will be suspending for the month of December. I need a plan to just get through these next two months.

Step Two: Affirm Your Stressless Future

My values haven't changed. What matters most to me is faith, friendship, and honesty. If I apply these values to the holiday stress I'm anticipating, what would my life look like? My faith will give me strength, especially where willpower is involved. A quick silent prayer helps when I'm tempted to binge on sweets or salty snacks. I love holiday parties, so I'm going to them! I'll try to focus more on the socializing and less on the eating. Need to come up with some strategies for that. I can also be honest if anyone gives me a hard time when I say no to desserts. I'll tell them I have diabetes and am trying to lose weight to manage the disease. I think they'll understand.

This is how I'm picturing myself at a cocktail party! I'm wearing my red silk dress and three-inch heels; I look fantastic! I fill my plate with the healthiest appetizers available. Hopefully there will be vegetable trays with hummus, cheese, and fresh fruit. I'll choose one small decadent dessert so I won't feel deprived and I'll eat it very slowly!

Affirmation: I am a healthy woman, living a vibrant, stress-free life and successfully managing my diabetes.

Step Three: Plan to Unravel Stress

My future story gives me some ideas for managing the stress over the holidays. Action items:

- *Dress in my best holiday attire so I feel beautiful! When I look good, I'm more self-confident. (4)*
- *Walk around the table to see what foods are available before selecting what to eat. (5)*
- *Fill my plate with the healthiest appetizers available. (5)*
- *Allow myself to choose two extra yummy appetizers and one small dessert. No more! (5)*
- *Eat slowly; take little bites; savor the food. (4)*
- *Limit myself to one glass of wine. Then switch to seltzer water with lime. (4)*
- *Stick to the plan; have a great time socializing; then reinforce my success by writing in my gratitude journal. (5)*

As I reflect on this list of action items, I feel excited about my plan. I think it's realistic and achievable. I've already had some success with changing my diet. I'm noticing I'm feeling more energetic and less sluggish. My clothes are even a little looser. I don't want to regain the eight pounds I've lost. This will be a challenge, but I'm ready for it!

SMART goal, based on 1 and 2 priority:

- **Specific:** *I will take stock of what's available to eat at all parties I attend before filling my plate with food.*
- **Measureable:** *I've achieved my goal when I successfully select veggies, cheese, and anything else that looks healthy.*
- **Achievable:** *I will accomplish this by asking my diabetes support group how they handle party food and what types of food they usually choose to avoid blood sugar highs.*

- *Realistic:* I will do this now because if I plan ahead I will know what to do when I see a table filled with yummy but fattening appetizers.
- *Time Bound:* I will complete this within the first hour of the party.

Step Four: Reflect and Commit to Destress

I know what to do about party food over the holidays but I'm also concerned about my exercise program. I've discovered that exercise really helps me manage my stress and diabetes. My blood sugar is always lower after a Zumba class. In fact, sometimes it goes a bit too low and I need to drink some juice to bring it back to normal range. The Zumba classes with Lucy have been so much fun! We laugh at lot and the teacher is great! I guess I can still commit to dancing over the holidays—just turn on some music and go for it! I believe there may be some online classes I can access. Just need to do a little research.

Here's my contract with myself:

I, Yvonne, agree to maintain a healthy lifestyle over the holidays by being conscious of my food choices when I attend a party and by continuing to exercise two days a week.

Signed, sealed, and delivered! Yvonne

Commentary

Yvonne is still on track with her diabetes and stress management. She's successfully negotiated three months since diagnosis and now has a strategy for getting through the holidays without sacrificing the joys of the season. Her writing reflects her optimism.

As she works her way through the four steps of Write to Be Well, Yvonne returns to her values as a way of reminding herself how her values can support her lifestyle changes. She weaves these values into a new vision of her future. She's even willing to picture herself in her red silk dress circling a table filled with tempting treats. After she reaffirms herself and her goals, she creates a specific action list to support her decision to maintain her diet plan while still enjoying the holiday season. In Step Four, she reflects on her plan, noting that she needs to address exercise. Although she does not resolve what to do, she does indicate she has an idea to investigate. She'll have to come back to this later and create exercise goals for the holidays. She concludes with a mini-contract with herself that highlights her commitment to maintain a healthy lifestyle.

By using Write to Be Well, Yvonne has averted what could be a minor crisis in her commitment to a healthy lifestyle. She has named her stress, expressed her feelings, come up with action steps, and made a commitment to herself. She is now prepared to manage the stress she associates with holiday eating.

ROUND THREE OF WRITE TO BE WELL

March: seven months after diagnosis.

Step One: Write Your Stress Story

Sleep or lack of it—that's what's stressing me out now. When my blood sugar's running high, I just can't sleep. I'm up every two hour, peeing. Then I can't get back to sleep. The next day I feel like a zombie and I can't think very clearly. I slog through the day, craving sweets. I feel like crap!

Step Two: Affirm Your Stressless Future

Values remain the same—faith, friendship, and honesty. Not sure how all these apply to my current situation. But if I'm going to be honest with myself, I need to admit I haven't been careful with my dinner meals lately. Should cut back on the carbs and increase veggies. If my blood sugar is high when I go to bed, perhaps I should do a few floor exercises to boost my metabolism. That might help.

Step Three: Plan to Unravel Stress

Action items:

1. *Limit carbs at dinner time. Max 15 grams. Stay away from choco-late and caffeine. (5)*

2. *Troubleshoot high blood sugar an hour before bedtime. Try doing sit-ups and planks. (4)*
3. *Get into bed by 10:30 pm. Relax, read, listen to quiet music. (4)*
4. *If I awaken during the night, test blood sugar, then read or do gentle stretches until I feel sleepy again. (3)*

Step Four: Reflect and Commit to Destress

I'm ready to try anything. This is a good start. I'll give my plan a month. If it doesn't work, I'm going to make a doctor's appointment to discuss whether I have sleep apnea.

Commentary

Yvonne confronts her latest stress honestly and directly. She spares no words in describing how she feels when she has a poor night's sleep. She doesn't linger in her anger but quickly acknowledges how her values help her face what she might do to change the outcome of a sleepless night. With this quick write, Yvonne hones in on what's important and what she can do to address her stress.

ROUND FOUR OF WRITE TO BE WELL

August: one year after initial diagnosis. Yvonne has successfully managed stress and diabetes for one year. She's lost fifteen pounds and kept it off. It's a slow process, but she's encouraged by the positive changes in the way she feels. She has more energy, and exercise helps to control her hunger, stress, and diabetes. Even her A1C, the blood sugar measurement doctors monitor, has improved. Over the year, Yvonne's set up a series of mini-goals and rewards to keep herself motivated. She keeps charts on the wall to record days that she's exercised and rewards herself with a spa day when she meets her monthly goals.

At the one-year mark, Yvonne agrees she has a lot to be thankful for, yet she's tiring of all the effort it takes to maintain her new lifestyle. She wants to shake up her routine to keep life interesting. Her journal entries speak about the challenges she's now facing. As you'll see, she spends more time writing at this one year mark. Still, she doesn't respond to every prompt but picks and chooses among the ones most pertinent at this stage in her life.

Step One: Write Your Stress Story

Prompt Two: Write Your Own Story

Diabetes is unrelenting! I feel like it's taken over my life. I'm exhausted from everything I must do to manage it. I'm tired of pricking my fingers to test blood sugar levels, counting carbs, and even exercising. I need to find a way to get psyched up again about caring for myself. I'm suffering from diabetes burnout!

Prompt Three: Shift Your Perspective

Lucy might notice I'm tired and depressed. This is what I think she'd say: It's been a year since Yvonne was diagnosed with diabetes. She's worked real hard to follow the recommendations of her diabetes team. She's exercising at the gym two days a week and coming with me to Zumba classes twice a week. I've noticed she's making healthier eating choices too. When we go out to lunch, she usually has a salad or fish. She's told me she cheats sometimes, but heck, she can't be perfect all the time. Maybe she needs to loosen up a bit, be more forgiving when she slips up in her routine. I know she's lost weight and she's looking good. We went shopping a couple of weeks ago; she was surprised that she'd dropped two whole sizes.

Notes to Self: Reflection

Maybe I do need to be more forgiving of myself. I get angry when my blood sugar is out of range. And that's not good. It just contributes to my stress! Even when I do my best, things still go wrong. It's really frustrating. Obsessing about my diabetes just adds to the burden of caring for myself. I probably need to talk with my diabetes educator to set up clear, reasonable, and reachable goals. Asking for support is always helpful.

Step Two: Affirm Your Stressless Future

Prompt One: Identify What Matters

When I did this prompt a year ago, I chose faith, friendship, and honesty as important values. I'm expanding the list to include appreciation, commitment, and fun.

What matters to me is appreciation because I want to take the time to appreciate my success and the other people who've helped me reach my goals.

What matters to me is commitment because managing stress and diabetes is a lifetime event requiring consistent commitment to a healthy lifestyle.

What matters to me is fun because I'm a fun-loving person who wants to enjoy the gifts of life!

Prompt Two: Write Your Future Story, Your Vision

I see myself maintaining my commitment to a healthy lifestyle. I'm exercising regularly and watching my weight drop an additional 15 pounds. When I reach my goal, I'm throwing a party. I'll invite Lucy and all the other people who have supported me on this journey to better health. Now that I have my weight under control, I'm able to manage my diet in social situations. I'm also writing regularly. In addition to Write to Be Well, I'm keeping a daily gratitude journal to offset the negativity I feel when I'm frustrated by diabetes.

Prompt Three: Write Your Affirmation

Affirmation: I am a healthy woman, living a vibrant, stress-free life and successfully managing my diabetes.

Notes to Self: Reflection

Yes, this feels good. I'm glad I added three new values to my list and revised my future story. Now I just need to figure out how to get there.

Step Three: Plan to Unravel Stress

Prompt One: Create Your Action Steps

1. *Buy a beautiful new writing journal for my gratitude pages. (3)*
2. *Find a new way to exercise. Maybe I'll try the spin class. Or maybe I'll get a pedometer and join a walking group. (4)*
3. *Make an appointment with diabetes educator and nutritionist. I need to tweak my diabetes goals and have the nutritionist review my meal plans. (5)*
4. *Plan one social outing each week. Reconnect with old friends. Try something new, like an art class at the local winery. (4)*
5. *Practice the art of forgiving myself. Let go and move on! It doesn't do me any good to wallow in self-pity! (4)*

Step Four: Reflect and Commit to Destress

It's been a year since I was diagnosed with diabetes. It's been a hard year, but I feel successful. I've lost 15 pounds and toned my body. I've learned I can change my dietary habits and not suffer. I'm eating healthier than ever before and enjoying my food. I will not gain back this weight!

I'm still participating in the diabetes support group. It's a good group of people. We encourage each other and celebrate our successes. But after a year it feels like it's time to mix it up a bit. I don't want to get bored with the diet and exercise plan I have in place. Diabetes burnout is a real threat. The disease is unrelenting. I think about it every day. So I'm hoping my new action steps will incentivize me, get me back on track and feeling optimistic again.

Commentary

Yvonne's had quite a journey this past year. When she was diagnosed with diabetes, it turned her life upside down. Suddenly, she stood face-to-face with her mortality. She had a choice. She could either embrace the challenge or give in to the disease, as her father did. She chose to live her life differently. In her journal entries, she admits the lifestyle changes haven't been easy. At times, she's felt discouraged and even feared she was suffering from burnout.

It takes a lot of effort to manage a chronic condition and the stress associated with it. Yvonne has used all the resources available to her— doctors, diabetes educators, nutritionists, exercise programs, support groups, her family and friends, and Write to Be Well. The professionals provided the guidance she needed to understand why diabetes threatened her life. Family and friends supported her in lifestyle changes. Write to Be Well challenged her to look within herself to find her way forward from diagnosis to thriving with diabetes. In a methodical way, the writing prompts challenged her to name her stress, write honestly about her feelings, identify her values, create a vision of an uplifting future, put an action plan into place, and commit to change.

Write to Be Well is the platform Yvonne needed to start and maintain her wellness journey. It helped her focus on what matters to her, what to do next, and how to meet the challenge. As her journal entries over the past year demonstrate, she turns to it again and again when she needs to confront and address new stressors that threaten to undermine her success.

10

GRIEF, DEATH, DYING, AND LIVING

Warren was married to his wife, Caroline, for over thirty-nine years when she suddenly died. They first met the summer before their senior year of high school through a mutual friend. They were instantly *in love* and inseparable. Their romance lasted as they dated throughout their college years, and the weekend after her college graduation, they married.

The years flew by, and their lives were filled with their growing family of three sons and a daughter. They were of different religious faiths and respectfully attended their own churches. The kids went to public schools and were raised in Caroline's church. Warren attended his church, and sometimes the family would join him for special occasions.

Like in many marriages, Warren and Caroline had limited time for each other with the demands and commitments of their kids, their activities, their work lives, and the sheer busyness of everyday life. He worked for a large insurance company for many years and was laid off when there was an economic downturn. He quickly landed another job and made a good enough living. Caroline convinced him to retire early, and with her pleading, he finally did.

One early morning about six months later, Caroline awoke with an excruciating headache. She sat up in bed, waking Warren. He helped her get out of the bed, but she was confused, said she couldn't see, and fell back down after losing her balance. Warren knew something was terribly wrong and dialed 911. The ambulance arrived quickly. It was too late though for Caroline, as she suffered a massive stroke and died that day.

Warren learned about Write to Be Well from a friend, Vince, who had participated in one of our test group workshops. After Caroline's death, Warren did some counseling with the pastor of his church, which he found somewhat helpful. He had also attended a church grief support group for a while. He confided in his friend Vince that he needed something but didn't know what it was to help him move forward. His friend suggested he try writing to help sort it out. Although Warren never considered himself "a writer," he decided to give it a try. Here are Warren's journal entries as he worked through the initial steps of using Write to Be Well and then continued to use the method to work through his priorities. This is Warren's story of grief and life that we share with you. From Warren's journal . . .

ROUND ONE OF WRITE TO BE WELL

Step One: Write Your Stress Story

Prompt One: Complete This Sentence Stem

The stressful situation (real or perceived) I am facing is *that I am lost. With Caroline gone, I just don't know what to do. Every day feels like I should be doing something that she would have been doing because she did it all and I went to work and brought home the money.*

Prompt Two: Write Your Own Story

> Write your story from the "I" perspective (first person), describing your thoughts and feelings surrounding the stressful situation, real or perceived.

I feel so horrible and every day I feel this way. I feel heavy and foggy. The kids are great. They invite me to dinner and to do things. Jake invited me to go down to Dallas and spend time with him and Brenda and the grandkids. That was good but I felt like a fifth wheel. I felt like they saw me as being weak that they had to invite me all the way there and check on me as if I couldn't deal with it all myself. Caroline used to handle everything. She made things happen. She loved the grandkids. Now she is gone, and I am doing my best to keep the house just like she would and to pay the bills on time and to get things for the grandkids just like she did. I feel horrible. It's like a sense of being weighed down by concrete. No, not weighed down by concrete but filled with concrete. I cry a lot. It's embarrassing. I was at the grocery last week and I ran into Caroline's good friend Karen. She was being kind asking how I was doing and how hard it must be for me without Caroline. I choked up and could barely speak. How embarrassing. I miss her so. Why did she die on me? I just don't know what to do with myself. Damn, why did I insist on working when she wanted me to retire early? Caroline wanted for us to make a list of trips, travel, have fun. She was always nagging me and I finally did retire after Laura finished college and we were clear financially with the kids. I kept saying no to traveling though—I wasn't ready to do that and accused her of spending too much money on stuff she bought the kids all the time let alone buying airlines tickets and traveling all over. Maybe I caused her stroke. Maybe she was harboring anger and frustration that could have been avoided if I hadn't been such a jerk. Things were kind of strained the week before she died. She was clearly pissed with me. Then again, I got pissed with her too. I just don't know what to do. I am so sad. I really do think it's all my fault. I deserve to feel this way. When I was seeing Pastor Fred after the funeral he said it was normal to feel this way. He's a good guy and I know he and others at church are here for me. So here I am—retired, no wife, no idea what to do every day and with the rest of my life. Even if I knew what to do, I just don't feel like it.

Prompt Three: Shift Your Perspective

Now write your story from another person's point of view (third person).

Warren is such a great guy. We've been friends for years. We've done so many projects at church together and shared lots of good times together with our families. I have sometimes felt like he is the brother I never had. Warren has taken Caroline's death really hard. Then again, who wouldn't having your wife wake up and die in your bed one day. Who's ready for that, ever? I see Warren struggling. We invite him for dinner or to go to a movie with us or something at church and he just says no.

It's no different than when Caroline was alive. Sometimes she would come to the potlucks and sometimes not.

What's the difference now? The things that he used to enjoy he just doesn't want to do anymore. He seems to be resisting them as if they would be disrespectful of Caroline. It's like he is hovering in a cloud and holding onto it so that he doesn't let go of her. While she is gone, her memories will always be here. Sort of like the marriage will continue but with the memories and not the real live person wallowing in grief and guilt.

He seems stuck and like he is blaming himself as if he killed her. He needs to recognize that she was a smoker and smoking isn't good for the old heart and blood vessels. It's not his fault. Warren is only 61 years old and has a long life ahead of him. I think about what Caroline would be doing now if it was Warren who had that stroke on that fateful day. She'd be out and about and moving on. She'd be doing things, going places, hanging out with her grandkids. I want to tell him that.

When we met for coffee the other day he said he felt like he was in a holding pattern. It was as if he needed a huge plan to be all figured out before he could move forward. He had so many times with tears in his eyes that I could see the pain and grief he is feeling. I told him to go talk to Pastor Fred again and asked about the grief group. I know he's a private guy and acknowledged that he doesn't feel comfortable with just talking to anybody to say how he feels. I am glad he has me to be here for him.

Notes to Self: Reflection

The following questions are a guide for your writing. Respond to those that are relevant to you in this moment.

1. What did you learn about yourself in responding to the prompts?
2. What did you notice about how stress plays out in your life? Did anything surprise you? Disappoint you? Annoy you? If so, be sure to name it!
3. What emotions did you uncover?
4. What happened in your body as you wrote? Did you experience any release of stress, or did you experience heightened anxiety?

5. Do you have clarity about the source of your stress, your thoughts, your feelings, and what they are "doing" to you? If not, you may want to go back and repeat the prompts.

This has been helpful to write this out. It's helped me to see what I am feeling as if through Vince's eyes—wow—sad, depressed, grieving maybe, and a bit guilty like it's my fault when it's not. I can see that I am stuck and caught up in feeling a bunch of things that Pastor Fred and I talked about—about Caroline dying—but I sort of didn't get it then. It was really helpful to put myself in Vince's shoes. Sort of made me admit some things that I wouldn't have otherwise. Denial? It's funny that I didn't think about any of this as stress until I saw this question here. But just writing it down and rereading it made my body feel different in a way that I wasn't aware of before. My shoulders aren't as grippy. Guess I am feeling stress and don't know it.

Commentary

Warren responds simply and authentically with the first prompt that asks what the stressful situation being faced is. He simply says, "I am lost." He then continues to elaborate on being lost by expressing what he feels. As we continue in his journal, it is clear that his being lost is the tip of the iceberg. As he tells his story, what this Step One is all about, he does so in a stream-of-consciousness mode. He is following the guidelines to ignore grammar and punctuation and to write for his eyes only. By doing so, he allows himself to express his feelings deeply, privately with himself, and to link those feeling to the events in his life. He also expressed perceptions he felt, an example being that on his trip to Dallas he thought his family saw him as weak. Whether real or imagined, expressing the emotion and linking it to the event that evoked that emotion will support his assimilation of Caroline's death into his life and his ability to process his grief and to move forward.

Warren also notes lots of details. For example, as he writes about the way Caroline wanted to travel, he also includes his response. The specifics he writes about help to complete the scenario that he is reliving.

Clearly, what Warren writes is meaningful to him. He uses the words "lost," "stuck," "heavy," "foggy," and "filled with concrete" to express the sadness and grief he is feeling. His writing helps him give what he feels a name so that he can do something about it. With the third-person story, he recognizes the stress he is feeling in his body with his "grippy shoulders" and by acknowledging that perhaps he has been in denial of the feelings and situation he is facing. Warren embraced the basics of expressive writing heartily in this Step One, and as we will see, it provides a solid foundation for him to find a way to his new future.

Step Two: Affirm Your Stressless Future

Prompt One: Identify What Matters

> List three important values threatened by stress. Then insert each value into this sentence stem to test why it matters: What matters to me is __ because __ .

1. *Family/friendship*
2. *Inner peace*
3. *Meaning*

Family and friendship mean everything to me. I need to belong and be part of their lives—the lives of the people I love. What good am I to them if I don't engage and get out and do things with them. The trip to Dallas. I was there but I wasn't really "there." I kept thinking about what I thought they thought rather than just being there and being with them all. I can see the difference now. And when Vince invites me to go with them, it's not out of pity, he's my friend and misses me just like I miss fun times with him.

Inner peace—I long for this. I want that physical feeling of cement to go away and the heaviness in my mind and heart to be lighter. I want to feel the peace that I felt when Caroline and I were together talking about the kids or planning something. Just being together. If I don't let myself feel at peace, how can I relate to anyone else?

Guess I think of it as purpose. Okay, on the list it's called meaning. Meaning matters to me because I need to feel like I am contributing somehow to something bigger than me. I worked all those years and it was meaningful to help people have insurance to protect them and their loved one's lives and homes, cars . . . There's meaning out there for me— I just need to find it beyond the kids and Vince and all.

Prompt Two: Write Your Future Story, Your Vision

> Write your future story, linking your values to your vision of life with reduced stress.

I've got the special keepsakes from our lives and pictures that bring back the memories of Caroline and my life together. They are on the shelves of the bookcase in the den. I go in there and talk to her now and then and that's okay. She's gone but not forgotten and I still love her so.

I've got my "Caroline plan" in place with the things I am doing with and for the grandkids. It's something she would have wanted to do, and I feel good about that. The girls have sure helped me figure out what to do about it.

I am not feeling the concrete anymore—it's been a few months without it. There's even a lightness that I feel—content? Maybe I will join the singles group at church. Singles, heh, it should probably be called the widow/widower people. I am also volunteering every week and using my financial skills to help people down at the community center. There's hope. . . .

Prompt Three: Write Your Affirmation

> Create an "I" statement of what you want to do, be, or achieve in the future: I am . . .

I am content with my life, involved with my family, friends, and community.

Notes to Self: Reflection

The following three questions are a guide for your reflection. Respond to those that are relevant to you in this moment.

1. Describe how your affirmation confirms your values and your desired future.
2. As you described your future story, name any emotions that arose and how they influenced you.
3. Are you ready to be guided in Step Three to write your plan to make your future a reality? If yes, you're ready to go. If no, revisit

your values, your future story, and your affirmation and modify as needed.

I wrote down my values and at first it was a short list. That didn't do it for me. After I reread them and wrote about why they mattered—it made a difference for me. The family and friends is part of the affirmation. That really matters cause that's the people I love and who Caroline loved too. It helps to feel that connection. Content . . . that is my inner peace. I like that word better. It feels right. Yeah, my affirmation is my future—that the people I love are part of it and I shed this lousy feeling and find contentment. What's next?

Commentary

In Warren's reflection, he demonstrates a critical element of Step Two by linking and acknowledging his values and how they relate to his vision of the future. His reflection also demonstrates how he connected his emotions with events. He is now able to feel more than overwhelming sadness, as demonstrated by him writing about the love he feels for family and friends and that it really matters to him.

While his writing about the future is brief, he provides sufficient detail to allow him to connect his values and feelings. Interesting to note is that he writes about the absence of the sadness he is currently feeling by expressing, "I am not experiencing the heaviness of the concrete anymore." In this way, you can see the value of naming the emotion of sadness, as concrete. The word *concrete* for him is the opposite of the contentment he envisions for his future.

The words Warren chose for his affirmation are simple and brief. It is a positive statement that depicts a high-level view of his future. The word *community* we interpret as his looking to connect with something bigger than himself. Let's see what becomes of that in the upcoming steps.

Step Three: Plan to Unravel Stress

Prompt One: Create Your Action Steps

> Write your affirmation from Step Two and create a list of the possible action steps you need for your affirmation to become a reality. Group like items, if any, and then assign a value of 1–5, with 5 being the highest priority.

- *Stop feeling so sad. (5)*
- *Talk to Pastor Fred. (5)*
- *Do the gratitude list Pastor Fred suggested. (4)*
- *Call the community center. (3)*
- *See what programs they have that I could be in. (4)*
- *Or see what programs I could lead. (2)*
- *Invite Joe and Carol for dinner at a restaurant—great neighbors. (3)*
- *Call Vince and thank him. Take them to dinner out. (3)*
- *Go to the church singles group. (3)*
- *Clean out Caroline's closet and all the stuff in the basement. (4)*
- *Figure out how to stop crying when people ask about Caroline. (5)*
- *Ask the girls to help me with the Caroline plan. (3)*
- *Make the keepsake space in the den. Find pictures I like. (4)*
- *Plan a trip. (2)*
- *Get rid of the concrete feeling. (5)*
- *Talk to the doctor about why Caroline died. (5)*
- *Figure out why I feel so guilty. (4)*
- *Get out of the house every day. (5)*
- *Talk to the kids and tell them what I am doing. (3)*
- *Go to Amoroso's to dinner—it will be hard but that was our special dinner place. (3)*
- *Decide—what do I do about my wedding ring. Is it weird to wear it? (2)*
- *Go see the doctor about my crying and pain in my stomach. (5)*

Now that I read this list of things and reread my stories, it's obvious that I am grieving. Grief, yes, that's it. I've read the books, articles, heard all about the process of grief—even the funeral director talked to me about it. Now I see that I need to let myself grieve, just be in it—they say—and move on to feeling some other way. I also see that I need to get a life. Life will never be the same. She is gone. I need to hold tight to the memories and learn how to live—again after all these years. I've got two big things to start with and then who knows how many more. But that's okay. One day at a time.

Prompt Two: Action Script Your SMART Goals

For your priority action, define your SMART goal by responding to the following sentence stems. It's okay to specify more than one goal; simply repeat the process.

SMART goal 1:

- **Specific:** *I will work to address my grief and feel content.*
- **Measurable:** *I'll know I've made progress when I have a next step.*
- **Achievable:** *Yes, I can write daily and call to make an appt. with Pastor Fred.*
- **Realistic:** *I have to make a change, now, to feel better. So, yes, I am not dreaming.*
- **Time Bound:** *I will write every day when I have coffee in the morning—before 9 am. I will meet with Pastor Fred in the upcoming week.*

SMART goal 2:

- **Specific:** *I will get a life.*
- **Measurable:** *In contrast to now, I will be out doing things.*
- **Achievable:** *Yes—respond to people's invites, get out and do it even if going through the motions.*
- **Realistic:** *Yes, I can do this and know that I might feel sad and teary. It's okay.*
- **Time Bound:** *I need a month from now to start.*

Notes to Self: Reflection

The following questions are a guide for your reflection. Respond to those that are relevant to you in this moment.

1. As I reflect on my goals, I (notice, think, feel, am surprised by, etc.) . . .
2. What do you hope will be the outcome of completing your goals?

Yes, I am ready. Seeing the times my list said to stop feeling sad, concrete . . . It's important and I have to get unstuck in the emotion that's dragging me down. I've never experienced anything quite like this before. When Mom and Dad died it felt so different. Then again, was it? I felt sad but they were older and not my wife. But there's a sameness to it. Here today and gone tomorrow. In the case of Caroline, here today and gone today. But I remember the sadness and the feeling of why didn't I do more for each of them and did I contribute to their dying in some way. Could I have been a better son? Yes, I worked through that and I can and will work through this. Family and friends and having inner contentment I can achieve. Otherwise—why bother living? There's a reason I am here. I am not giving up. Having meaning in my life will return. I will make it happen.

Commentary

Warren built a strong foundation in Steps One and Two by naming his emotions, articulating his values by not only listing them but also explaining why they mattered, along with expressing a possible vision for the future. While it is a small step, it is positive movement toward doing something to change his situation. In the third-person story he wrote in Step One, he said, "It was as if he needed a huge plan to be all figured out before he could move forward." It is clear that he recognized from that writing that he doesn't have to create a huge plan in order to move forward based on the vision he wrote about. By articulating two goals, first lessening the sadness and then getting a life, Warren has created small, achievable steps, with the underlying recognition that he doesn't have to do it all at once. In effect, he is giving himself permission with his writing to prioritize and take one step at a time.

Warren is clearly ready to move forward. This is evident as he expressed his next steps with positive words, for example, "I know" and "I can," and the absence of the word *but* in the statement, "Yes, I can do this and know that I might feel sad and teary. It's okay." Again, he is recognizing the feeling of sadness and tears, giving himself permission to feel that way in contrast to being teary and embarrassed by it, as in his Step One story. With his manageable action steps linked to his plan, he moves on to Step Four.

Step Four: Reflect and Commit to Destress

Prompt One: Explore Your Readiness

> Write in response to one or more of these questions to assess your willingness, belief, and commitment to move forward.

1. Are you confident in your ability to move forward? If yes, move on. If not, what do you need to feel more confident?
2. On a scale of 1 to 5, with 5 being the most important, how important is it for you to enact your plan? If a 4 or 5, move on, and if less than 4 or 5, explore why.
3. What do you believe about yourself and your ability to do this? Write it down; then dig deeply to explore if this belief holds true. If not, change it to reflect your inner truth.
4. Describe your attitude toward making the changes you've identified in your action plan. For example, are you pumped and ready to go, fearful, or . . . ?
5. Describe how you will hold yourself accountable. How will you reward yourself?

I just met with Pastor Fred. He was so reassuring and thoughtful. He encouraged me to keep doing what I am doing. I am even more encouraged that I will feel better and the gloom will eventually lift. I am confident. It feels good to write that.

I have to do this—otherwise I might as well quit living. I don't want to do that. Caroline wouldn't want me to do that. We had talked about that once or twice. What if one of us died? Horrible conversation but glad we did it. I need to tackle two things. Feeling happier down deep and getting a life. They go hand and hand and I need to start with feeling happier. When I get rid of the concrete I will have to find meaning and purpose—without Caroline. I will do this.

Prompt Two: Reflect on Your Plan

Write a letter to a trusted person and describe the following:

- What you're going to do (action plan),
- What you've learned about yourself to make it happen,
- Why you're committed,
- Any obstacles that may arise,
- What you will do about them.

Dear Vince,

You've been so helpful to me. You've been steadfast in helping me to deal with Caroline's death. Not pushy. Always there. Thanks, friend. I can't thank you enough for encouraging me to reach back to Pastor Fred, and to try this writing thing. I've been scribbling in one of those composition books I picked up at the Dollar Store. It's my private stuff.

It's become clear to me that I need to do two things. I need help to work through the overwhelming sadness that I feel. This feeling of concrete inside and the pain in my stomach. I have some work to do on that and I know it won't happen overnight, but I am going to keep writing and have already started to see Pastor Fred again.

I can see more clearly now that I am stuck and I know that you, my friend, and my family matter to me. I want to get back to living and this experience has helped me to see that a little bit at a time I will be able to get through this. Whatever comes up, I know that I have more fortitude than I give myself credit for having and that you and Pastor Fred and my family are all lifelines to help me.

Warren

Prompt Three: Contract for Change

Create a contract with yourself that positively states the key elements of your letter. Sign it, date it, and refer to it every day.

First: I will keep writing—I am going to repeat this for each of my goals. I will start tomorrow with gaining some feeling of contentment by writing and more follow-up with Pastor Fred. I give myself a month to start to feel better.

Second: I will get a life. At the milestone of completing the first—I will make a plan.

Notes to Self: Reflection

Reflect and write about what you are proudest of right now!

I feel like I've been wandering in the woods and now I have a path out. I am proud that I found that path.

Commentary

Warren was able to express his feelings by writing about the events that have occurred in his life. He then identified the depth of his sadness by eventually acknowledging that he was grieving. He had heard those words from other helpful sources, but until he connected what he was really feeling with his experience, he wasn't recognizing it necessarily as grief. By writing in his composition book, which only he read, he was able to more freely express his inner feelings without a fear of judgment or embarrassment whether he cried or not.

His third-party story was a breakthrough for him, based on a conversation he shared with us. He said that making observations of himself from his friend Vince's viewpoint was a wake-up call. He was able to recognize that part of his being stuck was the fact that he was enabling himself by not accepting the invitation of friendship from Vince and the love of his family to help him move forward. By identifying his value of family/friendship, he realized that he was denying the very people who mattered most to him in his life. An example of this is Warren's writing about his time in Dallas with his son and family. By expressing that he felt weak and unable to accept their care and concern, he recognized his inability to be fully present with them.

When Warren saw his brainstormed list in writing, he recognized the repetition of feeling sad and needing to get a life. He was able to see these as two big areas of focus. With this discovery, he felt comfortable continuing his writing and returning to Pastor Fred to help him work through his grief and move on. His commitment to writing helped him to continue expressing himself privately and then seek support as he felt comfortable.

What follows here is Warren's continued use of Write to Be Well to address his two priority areas. He starts by working on his first contract with himself to address his sadness. He chose to write every day for a month by following the basic steps and also choosing which prompts he wanted to write about that day. You will see that he uses some prompts and reflections as guidance rather than following them verbatim. On some days, Warren repeated certain prompts where he felt it was helpful for him to sort out what he was feeling. He used his writing to help him articulate himself in his sessions with Pastor Fred. Presented here are some, but not all thirty, of the writing responses he completed during the month that he committed to keep writing to move toward a feeling of contentment.

ROUND TWO OF WRITE TO BE WELL—WARREN'S FIRST GOAL

Step One: Write Your Stress Story

Okay—so—here's the first commitment I made with myself.

So it's not really a stressful situation anymore—at least I don't think so. First, I will keep writing every day for a month. It's been so helpful to write down what I feel. I feel lighter. It makes it real and reminds me that it's okay to work through my grief. I need to do it. I am committed to my affirmation. I have it on a sticky note on my bathroom mirror. And I will write it here every morning with coffee.

I am content with my life, involved with my family, friends, and community.

Prompt Two: Write Your Own Story

From the time I was a little kid, I was always the responsibility magnet, taking on whatever needed to be done—usually for someone else. I remember when Van Smith got sick and I blamed myself for pushing him to eat the whole bag of licorice. I grew up in a happy family but we sure didn't have much to fall back on financially. Dad and Mom worked hard. I worked so hard all my life too, to be sure that Caroline and the kids were well provided for. I was being responsible for sure by not retiring and going off and spending money in the way Caroline wanted me to do. When I read back through all my writings, I can see that I was blaming myself for Caroline's death. Thinking I caused it. Sort of like the licorice with Van. I didn't make him sick—it did. I sure contributed to it, but then again, he could have said no or stopped eating it. Just like Caroline could have stopped smoking. I nagged her about that just the way she nagged me about retiring.

Prompt Three: Shift Your Perspective

Okay—what does Pastor Fred see in me when we talk? Warren is a good man who worked hard to provide for his family. He loved his wife deeply and cared about her. He is understanding more clearly the natural stages of grief and that it takes time to heal. I think he's gotten the message that it's a big deal for your spouse to die and it's an even bigger deal for it to happen so suddenly. I think he's now seeing that while he can feel guilty about how he might have contributed to her death, he did not cause her death. He feels guilty that he didn't join her church as she wanted him to. He didn't retire when she wanted him to. He is beginning to understand it's okay to feel guilty and good to forgive himself and by doing so he will be letting go of those things in the past that are contributing to his sadness.

Notes to Self: Reflection

I am human. My past helped shape who I am today. I am a good man who loved and still love my wife. I didn't cause her death. I need to stop thinking I did. I need to stop feeling that I did. I forgive myself.

Step Two: Affirm Your Stressless Future

I value family/friendship, my inner peace, and a life of meaning.

It feels good to write these things that matter to me every day. This and my affirmation. I am content with my life, involved with my family, friends, and community.

Every day I am choosing to move closer to being content with my life and involved with my family, friends, and community. I am taking the time to feel the sadness and then moving forward with the day. Doing the little SMART thing every day even for a tiny task. The inner peace is coming. I forgive myself for feeling selfish about retirement. I didn't *cause Caroline's death. I just wish we had talked through things more. We didn't. That's the past and I am letting it go. My family and friends are here and now. Keeping Caroline's memory alive is important to me.*

Prompt Two: Write Your Future Story, Your Vision

I wrote about creating the keepsakes shelf and proud that I've done it! I had to clear out the books to make room. It was hard going through the photo albums and choosing the pictures that I wanted to display. In the future—I'll enjoy changing these pictures to keep the memories alive. It's Christmas and it's fun to see Caroline and the kids in front of the tree.

Prompt Three: Write Your Affirmation

I am content with my life and involved with my family, friends, and community .

Step Three: Plan to Unravel Stress

I need to work on the "Caroline plan." Truth of the matter is—I probably wouldn't have been involved in it if she were alive. But I am actually feeling happy about this as if we were doing it together. Okay—here's the plan for today to make this happen. Yeah, yeah, the SMART thing.

Prompt Two: Action Script Your SMART Goals

- **Specific:** *I will create a calendar with the kids' birthdays and holidays when I am going do something for them or with them.*
- **Measurable:** *I can know it's done when I have it filled in.*
- **Achievable:** *I can use Caroline's book and call the girls for ideas of things to get or do.*
- **Realistic:** *Yes—it will be fun to go out and shop for them and set up the dates.*
- **Time Bound:** *I will finish this plan by the end of today.*

Notes to Self: Reflection

I am glad I am doing this. I feel happy and it'll be fun to surprise the kids.

Step Four: Reflect and Commit to Destress

Prompt Two: Reflect on Your Plan

Dear Me,

It's day 27. Looking back on the month I can see that I am moving myself forward by writing about what I am going to do today. Doing the SMART thing with big and little stuff. I've made the keepsake corner, I've made the calendar, I've even bought some of the things for the kids' birthdays. It's been good to get out. I realize I am committed to healing from this tragedy and it's okay to feel sad, then move on. No guilt about that.

Prompt Three: Contract for Change

I've made it—it's day 30. With the help of Pastor Fred and my writing I am allowing myself to grieve and I am learning to let go of the sadness while I focus on doing something that matters to me for my family. My next contract is to move on to the second goal. I need to move on with my life. One step at a time. I can do it.

Notes to Self: Reflection

I am proud of myself—but not boastful. I am not going to wallow in sadness. I am going to accept it and learn to live again. I've already started.

ROUND TWO OF WRITE TO BE WELL—WARREN'S SECOND GOAL

Step One: Write Your Stress Story

The stressful situation I am facing is that I was feeling lost, not knowing how to live without Caroline. Now that I see a path, it's stressful to think about making a new life for myself, just me, alone. But I do have my family and friends cheering me on—because I let them.

Prompt Two: Write Your Own Story

Caroline and I were together forever. I can't really remember living without her. Living as a kid wasn't really living alone cause Mom, Dad, and my brothers and sisters were always in the picture. This is daunting. To live my life as an adult in a new and different way. Nothing is the same. Life will never be the same without her. What is it they say, what's the new normal? Well I've got to make a new normal and make a life of my own. Feels selfish but I know in my heart it isn't. She is gone and by moving forward I am not disrespecting her. I am afraid of venturing out. I cannot imagine dating. Bill at church started going out with other women not too long after his wife died. That's him, not me. Okay, so what is me?

Prompt Three: Shift Your Perspective

Warren's doing so much better. He doesn't seem as sad and is open to getting out and doing things. We talked the other day about his never having really lived as an adult by himself because he and Caroline were always together from high school days onward. While he says he is afraid, I see a hint of curiosity and almost sense of adventure in his eyes and hear it in what he talks about. I think he is excited to explore some new things that he wouldn't have done otherwise now that he has free time to do it. He is seeing that he is adjusting not only to Caroline's absence but also to the change brought by retiring.

He mentioned Bill dating and that's not for him. I think he sees Bill as trying to replace his wife. He's talked about getting involved in some community things. He told me all about the calendar with the kids and grandkids. It makes me happy to see he is doing things on his own that he wouldn't have done before. He did that with his family situation and now he is going to make it happen with what he is calling "getting a life." I am excited for him.

Notes to Self: Reflection

Writing these third-party-view things is really meaningful for me. Funny how putting the words on paper that express what I am thinking is so much easier when I have someone else saying them. It's easy for me to write what I think Vince sees. I am lucky he is my friend.

Step Two: Affirm Your Stressless Future

My core values are

1. *Family/friendship*
2. *Inner peace*
3. *Meaning*

What matters most to me right now is meaning. I want to give back to the greater good. I know my life has meaning to be present and available to my family and friends. This is a different kind of meaning. To do meaningful things and help make a difference in the world and for other people.

Prompt Two: Write Your Future Story, Your Vision

I am happier now than I've been in years. I feel good about the changes I've made in my life. I miss Caroline still and know that she'd be happy that I've moved on. In addition to the time I spend with each of the kids' families, I am volunteering two days a week with Habitat for Humanity. I really enjoy working with the other guys and the variability of the tasks and projects. They've talked to me about maybe being a project lead sometimes. It feels good to have my management skills recognized. It's awesome to help someone have a home of their own who couldn't otherwise. Talk about giving to the greater good and having meaning in my life. Also, I am about to decide on taking guitar lessons or singing lessons. It will be one or the other. I've always wanted to do this and maybe help me with my sense of peace.

Prompt Three: Write Your Affirmation

I am happy and living life to the fullest with my family, friends, and community.

Whoa—*this is a big gulp to let go of my old affirmation and step it up. I am moving on to this new affirmation.* I am happy and living life to the fullest with my family, friends, and community. *There, I've said it again. The first affirmation isn't extinct. It helped me to get me where I am today. I've gone from affirming being content to being happy. For some, that's nothing. For me it feels* big. *I see a highway moving forward.*

Step Three: Plan to Unravel Stress

Affirmation: I am happy and living life to the fullest with my family, friends, and community.

Action items:

- *Keep up what I am doing about contentment. (5)*
- *Make social appointments—out to dinner invites. I can't cook worth beans. (3)*
- *Go to Habitat and sign up. (5)*
- *Make an appointment at the music school and explore trade-offs of singing or guitar. (5)*
- *Review that first task list I made and cross off what I've done. (4)*

Prompt Two: Action Script Your SMART Goals

- **Specific:** *I will start doing music and Habitat.*
- **Measurable:** *I will get each scheduled.*
- **Achievable:** *I want to do this. I will do this. Yes, this is achievable cause I've already had some contact with them. I just need to seal the deal.*
- **Realistic:** *I've researched it. Yes.*
- **Time Bound:** *Starting next week.*

Notes to Self: Reflection

By doing this SMART thing it's like a list for me and something that I can focus on, get the satisfaction of doing something. Then I sit back and look at where I've been and what I am doing and I feel happier. I am taking the time to grieve. Sitting and letting the tears flow. Then getting on with my SMART thing for the day. It is keeping me going. In two weeks I will have my work with Habitat up and going.

Step Four: Reflect and Commit to Destress

Dear Kids,

I love you each. This has sure been a rough time to get through. I can't thank you enough for all of your help and support. Sorry if I haven't been there enough for you all too. You had a big loss too.

I've told you all about this but, to say it again, I have been working on finding happiness without Mom and am feeling that contentment grow. Please don't misunderstand what that means. It is that now I am working to get a life without her and still deeply in love with her. In the next two weeks I am going to be out volunteering with Habitat and also doing some music lessons. Don't worry, I will still have plenty of time for us to get together too. I have momentum going and surely will have some kind of setback along the way. Sometimes the sadness still overwhelms me. I have learned how to manage it and move on.

Thanks—I love you. Dad

I will

- *do a gratitude list daily*
- *do Habitat twice a week*
- *take the singing lessons and join the choir*
- *keep writing and sharing*

Notes to Self: Reflection

It's been a year since Caroline died. I am living my affirmation and proud of it.

I am happy and living life to the fullest with my family, friends, and community.

Now that I am so proud of myself—it's time to set a new goal and see what comes next.

Commentary

Warren is on a solid path moving forward with his life as he chooses to. While not considering himself a writer, he certainly did write and respond to the prompts. His openness and ability to write what he was feeling by connecting it to what he was experiencing was key. From the start, he allowed himself to name his emotions in the privacy of his journal. Through his writing, he allowed himself to express deeply the pain he felt, name it, and then work to manage it and the underlying stress it created in his mind and body.

He followed the method closely at first and then found what worked for him moving forward. The SMART goals step combined with his values and affirmations was his guide. As he developed the habit of writing regularly, he was able to pick and choose what felt right in the moment to work with. The scalability of the Write to Be Well method is demonstrated by Warren's recognizing he had a complex situation to address. With his writing in Step Two, he broke it down to two initial parts that were manageable. His closing entry shows the evolution of his affirmation and that he recognizes he is ready to move on to tackle another step in the process of healing fully from his grief and to embrace life!

Section 4

Stay Well

The Write to Be Well Lifestyle

Lifestyle is the way you choose to behave on a day-to-day basis. It includes the activities you engage in, the attitudes and opinions you express, the interests you pursue, the values you live by, and even the way you choose to allocate your income. The key word here is *choose*. We have a choice to live according to our values. Sometimes it's not easy, especially if we've lost sight of what really matters most to us. Life can get complicated. Stress can tip the scale, pulling us away from our good habits, if we don't manage it. Then, before we know it, we're spiraling into a lifestyle that doesn't support our health and positivity. It takes time and commitment to live according to our values and choices, and when necessary, to turn an undesirable habit into one that complements our well-being.

Our goal when we adopted the Write to Be Well lifestyle was to "get well, be well, *stay well*," and I imagine it's one of your goals too. We know that when we don't feel our best life gets out of sync, and even the little stressors can feel like big hairy audacious problems! Write to Be Well has always kept us on track with feeling our best by helping us own up to behaviors we want to change—and, even more importantly, take action to make the change happen! The widely held premise about behavior change is this: change happens when the pain of staying the same is greater than the pain of change.[1] Author Anais Nin expressed this well in saying, "And the day came when the risk to remain tight in a bud was more painful than the risk it took to blossom."[2] It was when we each had a serious health threat that writing became even more important in our lives and why later we developed the Write to Be Well method. Now it's a part of our lifestyle. We find Write to Be Well helps us turn around our pain and continue building the life we desire.

In the previous chapters, you learned how to apply the four-step Write to Be Well method to your stressful situations. You read the journals of four people with diverse issues and saw how they tweaked the method to fit their needs. And you read about the many years of research that proves writing heals. The big question for you now is understanding your *why*.

Why change? Why invest the time? Simon Sinek, author of *Know Your Why*, equates *why* to purpose. He says the discovery of your personal *why* is an *aha* moment.[3] For many who've used Write to Be Well, the *aha* moment comes when you work with your personal values. People find that by naming their values, they're reminded of what's most important to them. It prompts them to get their life back in alignment with their values, which restores their passion for life.

Write to Be Well is a lifestyle choice. Think of it as another tool in your arsenal of options for managing stress. The four steps can stand alone as a way of monitoring stress and what you intend to do about it, or help you sustain your good habits. It can also be used in conjunction with your other stress-management tools, such as exercise, nutrition, meditation, and relaxation techniques.

The decision is up to you. Will you accept the Write to Be Well challenge and make writing part of your lifestyle or at least try it? It's as easy as one, two, three, four! In the next two chapters you'll learn how to turn the four steps into a habit and how to make this writing method work for you. Chapter 11 shows you what it takes to achieve long-lasting behavior change with intention, understanding of change transitions, and how to establish desired habits. Chapter 12 shows you how to enrich your Write to Be Well lifestyle by keeping the passion for writing alive with writing groups, writing partners, and alternative prompts! When you choose the Write to Be Well lifestyle, you'll find writing keeps you focused on managing your stress to achieve healthy outcomes. We hope you'll join us in writing to get well, be well, *stay well*!

11

BUILD YOUR HABIT WITH INTENTION

In our professional lives, we've helped clients embrace the opportunity to achieve desired and lasting change to improve their lives. We've accomplished this from our different perspectives and expertise and found a strong commonality. Most of our clients expressed a need or desire to change their situation; some were very clear about what that change would mean for them, while others simply had to change their situation because the pain was no longer tolerable.

In each instance, we found four key elements of success: newfound awareness, an image of the future, intention, and persistence. The proven tools and methods we provided helped them see in new and different ways what, why, and how they needed to make a change. We supported them in exploring and discovering for themselves what the image of the future looked like. We provided encouragement and feedback to help them shape their intention and continue to achieve their goal, as the answer for each person's desire lies within them. We believe no one can tell you what that is or how to do it, but we can certainly support you on your journey with Write to Be Well.

In the same manner as with our counseling and consulting clients, Write to Be Well provides a set of proven tools, in an integrated and repeatable method, that scales to address large, small, chronic, or one-time issues. These tools help you discover, on your own, what you need and desire to tame your stress and live a healthier life.

Keeping in mind the instructions and stories presented in previous chapters on how to use Write to Be Well, our challenge is for you to make this writing practice a natural part of your self-care. You may already have items that you rely on to manage stress; perhaps meditation, exercise, or breathing techniques. Maybe you have a stress ball on your desk that you can squeeze when the going gets tough. These are certainly beneficial practices that may provide immediate relief of tension. Our challenge is a different kind of stress relief. It is a lifestyle of writing that is action oriented to address your issue(s) with precise steps to achieve desired change. It is an ongoing, dedicated path to maintain lasting behavioral change that makes a difference for you. To enhance your journey with Write to Be Well, this chapter provides background information about change, intention, and making new habits, as well as some cutting-edge perspectives on brain science.

CHANGE

So you've decided quietly, or perhaps with a big *aha*, that you are ready to commit to writing as a stress-reducing lifestyle and make a change in your life. Congratulations, we applaud you! Maybe the change is about confronting someone who you feel is persistently undermining you at work, changing your job, addressing nitpicky things that bug you, or maybe adjusting your attitude about your chronic health condition. Whatever it is, your first step is simply to recognize this as a change.

There is good news in the longstanding body of psychological research about human behavior that supports the belief we have an innate ability to make lasting behavior change. The framework for Write to Be Well is based on this premise and the works of noted psychologists William James, Carl Jung, Carl Rogers, Alfred Adler, Abraham Maslow, and Martin Seligman, among others. For the purpose of brevity, here is a summary of their beliefs and premises:

- James: We have positive innate qualities that support us every day.
- Jung: By working toward a future orientation we can draw ourselves in that direction.
- Rogers: The value of self-disclosure can be enhanced by a client-centered relationship. With Write to Be Well your writing is an

important form of self-disclosure that is foundational to behavior change.

- Adler: We are creators and artists of our own lives.
- Maslow: When we remove the barriers in our lives, we empower ourselves to move to higher and higher levels of self-actualization.
- Seligman: We innately want to lead meaningful lives and can cultivate and enhance this through, among other things, a focus on positive emotions and our strengths instead of what we view as weaknesses.[1]

With this positive grounding for making change in our lives, let's consider the process we go through to be fully comfortable with a new behavior or situation.

Change is often described as hard, but what does this really mean? Once the decision is made, we believe it's the transition to achieve that change that is most difficult. William Bridges's Transition Model of Change supports this thinking with its three stages: Endings, the Neutral Zone, and New Beginnings.

As humans we each experience change in different ways. In the context of Bridges's Transition Model, let's explore the deeper meaning of each stage so you can decide for yourself how *you* experience change and which stage is most challenging for you. By developing an awareness of your pattern of behavior in a change transition, you will be better positioned to be intentional and less stressed in achieving your goal.

The first stage, Endings, is the process of acknowledging what you are losing, or giving up, rather than being engaged with what is new. This is a period of uncertainty as you recognize what you are letting go of and begin adapting to the new environment or routine. Buying a new home is an example. You may feel jubilant about the prospect of your new home while at the same time feel reservations or even denial about making the move. As you acknowledge what you are giving up, you move to the middle stage of the process, the Neutral Zone. With this stage it is natural to feel anxiety, excitement, or even denial as you question and perhaps reexamine your decision. This is a time when the old situation no longer exists, but you are not fully functioning in your new situation either. Some people get stuck here and never move on. We recall a client who sold their home in the northeast part of the

United States and moved to Florida. Because they continually longed for the life and home they left behind, they never let go of it to make room for new friends or experiences. They said they hated living in Florida but never really engaged with their new environment. They eventually decided to sell their home in Florida and move back to New Jersey. Effectively, they never let go of their old way of life, doubted their decision, and never left the Neutral Zone! Their being stuck there emotionally and psychologically kept them from realizing a dream they had worked toward for years.

By acknowledging potential feelings of confusion and doubt, you allow yourself to be energized and grow in your new situation. Only then can you enter the last stage of change transition, which Bridges refers to as New Beginnings. In this stage you gain new insights, attitudes, and ways of doing things. You might experience a feeling of exuberance and a fresh sense of identity while you revisit and fine-tune your goals and values. Recognizing the stages and associated feelings during a transition allows you to move forward and successfully accomplish your desired change.

Let's consider the scenario of deciding if the companionship of a dog is meaningful for you before you bring home a rescue puppy. While it is a desired change that you've looked forward to, taking time to recognize what you're giving up is important. You can no longer stay away from home for hours or days on end without making provision for your pet's exercise, bathroom routine, and meals. Feelings that may arise could be sadness or even anger due to loss of freedom. Recognizing what you need to give up beforehand will help you be successful in the transition with your furry friend. Similarly, before you are settled in with your new pet, you may be annoyed by certain events. This is the Neutral Zone experience. Self-doubt about your decision and reevaluation might occur. Recognizing that these thoughts and feelings may naturally arise again will help you manage the transition from petless to happy dog owner. Then the third phase arrives, and you are settled in and content with your new companion. You find walking with him or her and the unconditional love a pet can provide are stress relievers for you. This is a New Beginning that deserves celebration.[2]

The question is, how have you experienced change in the past? Take a moment to write about a change that you lived through.

- Describe the process you went through to make the initial decision. Did you agonize over it, ruminate with it, or quickly arrive at the commitment to make a change? Did you consider what you would be giving up?
- How did you explore what would be different for you as a result of this change? Think about whether you second-guess your decisions or have difficulty letting go of your old way of living.
- Did you have a clear picture in your mind of what success looked like so that when you achieved it you could declare victory?

It's important to be aware of how you move through the change process and the outcome you've achieved. Now, for future reference, reflect on which part of transitioning is hardest for you.

LIVING INTENTIONALLY

A famous quote from Pulitzer Prize–winning author Annie Dillard resounds in the many discussions about living with intention: "How we spend our days is, of course, how we spend our lives."[3] When I first read this quote, it had a profound impact on me. I began thinking about how we get up every morning and execute the activities of our day, day after day, which adds up to our life—a life that we perhaps believe is one that never ends. Then you hear about a friend, a relative, or someone in the news who dies suddenly, and the wake-up call rings with the message that life is not forever. This sounds a bit morbid and dramatic perhaps, yet it gets our attention.

So the question is, how do we live and make every moment count while feeling, and being, the best we want to be? Living life intentionally is a choice we each can make. It requires us to be purposeful and thoughtful about what we do and how we do it. It is about adopting a lifestyle that supports us in not merely passing the days but living them to the fullest in the best way possible.

So the choice is yours. Being stressed out in a situation that you don't want to be in offers you a choice to change your behavior and your attitude about what you are dealing with, or perhaps change the situation. You have the choice to be intentional about what you do and also how you do it. Living a life that has meaning and purpose is truly an intention you can choose to pursue, or not. It requires an awareness of what matters to you, the vision of what you want your life to be, and the will to make the change. Write to Be Well helps you define this for yourself. The choice is yours to be intentional about making it happen, with Write to Be Well as a central part of your stress management tool set.

Reflect on your intention to take the challenge with Write to Be Well and take a moment to write about it. Christopher Reeve was Superman in his movie role and a super man with intention in his life after becoming paralyzed. For me, he inspires intentionality with this quote: "So many of our dreams seem impossible, then they seem improbable, and then when we summon the will, they soon become inevitable."[4]

HABITS

Habits are powerful. There are good habits and bad habits depending on how you judge them. A good habit could be brushing your teeth multiple times in the day and being compelled to do so without thinking. A bad habit might be driving erratically every day on the way home from your work when you encounter heavy traffic, increasing the odds of a fender bender. Habits are essentially patterns of behavior that we may or may not be aware of. My mom loved to have treats and goodies to eat at her home, available for anyone who visited. She had a habit of regularly purchasing what she offered in the way of nuts, sweets, and savory snacks whether she had one, two, or more backups on the shelf. On the recipient side of the treats, it became a family trait to walk into Mom's house and immediately begin snacking on something, whether offered or not. The cue was simply entering the house and being greeted by Mom! No choice in the matter needed to be considered; it was automatic.

Another way to consider a habit is something you do, most likely repeatedly, without making a choice. For those I've known who have talked about their experience of quitting the use of tobacco products, the resounding challenge is the habit of lighting up on some cue. The cue is perhaps pouring a cup of coffee, receiving a phone call, or getting into the car. There is no deliberate choice made to smoke; rather, it is just habit. Another example is when we each get up in the morning. There is undoubtedly a series of actions that each of us enacts simply out of habit. This allows us to be on autopilot and accomplish many aspects of starting the day quite efficiently, or perhaps puts us on a slippery slope of actions that we really don't want to happen at all.

The question is, how do we harness the power of habits to support a desired change in our lives? If you are thinking you need to eliminate a habit, know that it is a tall order, repeatedly shown to be pretty impossible to achieve. Consider instead that you have the ability to *alter* your habit and support your intention successfully. Let's consider why.

Say you have a goal of eating healthy food and shedding some extra pounds. Most every afternoon at the office you begin to feel tired, cranky, and stressed around 3:30. Remember, a habit starts with a cue, results in a reward, and in the middle of those two elements is a routine. Your brain translates the 3:30 feelings as hunger, which is the cue for you to do something routinely. Your reward is shifting your emotions to feel better by getting out of your chair, taking a stretch break, and energetically feeling more satisfied. Now the question is the pattern of behavior in the middle. The routine is to get up, walk to the vending machine and grab a candy bar, and eat it without thinking about it.

With awareness and focus, the routine pattern of behavior in the middle of the cue and reward can be changed into a healthy choice that supports you in achieving your goal. By recognizing your feeling each day, let's call it the hunger cue, you can focus on the choice of snack you wish to eat. Instead of the candy bar, you can thoughtfully choose a peanut butter cracker from the vending machine. By changing the routine behavior, you transform or replace the habit rather than eliminate it. By keeping the cue and reward intact, it helps you to make the change. By being intentional in taking small, focused steps with your routine pattern of behavior, you empower yourself to successfully achieve your ultimate goal with gradual change. The switch from the choice of a candy bar to peanut butter crackers isn't a radical change. It is one small step on your way to a new pattern of behavior that will support you in achieving your ultimate goal of healthy eating.

To establish Write to Be Well as a lifestyle tool to manage your stress and reach your desired future and goals, create a habit by setting up a cue, a reward, and a routine that works for you. Your cue could be what you feel is the best time of day to write. Many people write first thing in the morning to set a positive tone and intention. We know some who prefer to write at the close of each day to sort out their feelings, reflect on their actions, and get ready for the next day. Others prefer to write at a set time during the day or perhaps take time out when their stress builds. You decide what works for you. The reward is supporting yourself to achieve the goals and lifestyle you desire. The routine is your choice of where, when, and how you make time to write. What is important is for you to decide what works best and be intentional about following your cue and recognizing when you need to adjust your routine to best suit your circumstance.

There are two final points about habits: the role our brains play, and the power of believing you can achieve your goal. It's proven that our brains reinforce the routine patterns of behavior that are our habits. Walking is a big part of my exercise regimen. I walk five days a week. If I don't, I have a craving for it and feel like I will explode if I don't hit the road first thing every morning.

Researchers monitoring the brain waves of monkeys have found our brains perform two key actions with habits. The first is the neurological activity normally seen when a reward is obtained. A monkey was presented with a shape on a computer touch screen, and if they chose the correct shape, a reward in the form of juice was provided. With each instance of selecting the right shape and reward, the monkey's brain showed a neurological spike suggesting happiness. The selection behavior became a habit, as demonstrated by the monkey being more and more practiced in the behavior. What followed, the second key action, was most interesting for researchers: as the pattern of behavior became stronger, the neurological spike of reward began to occur *before* the juice was given as a reward.

Further experiments performed by a variety of researchers varied the timing of the reward, the degree of habit developed in relation to the reward, and other factors. The net conclusion provides insight into how habits create neurological cravings. These cravings most likely occur gradually, leaving us unaware they are developing. Once developed through habit, our brains push us to repeat the routine that results in the reward we crave. If we add this neurological craving to the earlier scenario of the 3:30 candy bar, the importance of keeping the reward intact and modifying the behavior is important to note. Our brains are not programmed at first to have an afternoon candy bar. It is the habit of routinely eating the candy bar in the same way that perpetuates our old behavior. Being aware of what maintains your habits and being focused on modifying your routine behavior gradually will serve you well. To modify and develop new habits, the golden rule is to keep the same cues and rewards; then focus on changing the routine behavior in the middle.

The precise results we each have in enacting change will vary based on our uniqueness. In order to maintain a modified or new habit, it is essential for you to believe it is possible. When working alone, you can successfully discover what and how you want to change, but whether you believe you can or not is critical. Participation in a writing support group has been proven to increase your likelihood of believing you can make a change. The belief that change is possible is reinforced by learning what similar challenges and successes others have experienced. We provide more information about writing support groups in chapter 12.[5]

NEUROSCIENCE AND BEHAVIOR CHANGE

Earlier we talked about the role of fight or flight and stress as they relate to our drive to survive. This is our reality. Not necessarily connected to our reality are three basic human drives:

- Being in control of our individual destiny,
- Learning about our environment so we can find stability and predictability in our lives,
- Avoiding pain and discomfort.

In striving for these things, we are regularly and consistently bombarded by stress that threatens our ability to achieve any or all of our goals. At the same time, change is constantly happening in our surroundings, our minds, and our bodies, whether we are aware of it or not. How we reconcile this tension in order to cope with stress and change our behaviors is found in the cutting-edge area called neuroscience. Understanding the basics of neuroscience helps in understanding how each step of Write to Be Well as a lifestyle tool supports you in achieving your goals.

Behaviors shape our brains. This happens physically when neurons form to create neural pathways. To get a little technical about what is happening in our brains, as neurons connect to other neurons, they are called dendrites. Dendrites then connect to each other and increase as behaviors are performed in an established and frequent way. Eventually, the neural pathway keeps perpetuating the behavior without our even thinking about it.

If we consider this in the context of our discussion about habit, unwanted behaviors are preserved through both the neural pathways habits create and the cravings we feel. If we consider this in the context of creating new habits, it's highly encouraging that we can create new pathways and new behaviors!

In simple terms, you can think of it as rewiring your brain. It is also referred to as brain stickiness. This science is based on the knowledge that when information is filed away as important, as in the values you identified in Step Two of Write to Be Well, it makes a difference in supporting behavior change. By building new brain cell connections, in as many areas of the brain as possible, these pathways perform with greater efficiency over time so that our actions become automatic and habitual. Our brains do not store all the information about a particular behavior in one place. Rather, the information can be stored in multiple locations, further strengthening the new behavior.

Brain stickiness is supported in Write to Be Well by your writing about your emotions, insights, actions, meaningful values, and envisioned future in the form of an affirmation! The positive use of words to express emotion helps to support change. The amygdala in our brains regulates emotion and interacts with areas that govern our cognitive function and awareness. Positive words used in reflections support movement toward change, resulting in an increase in health and reduction in stress.

To create a new habit, it is estimated that ten thousand repetitions are needed for a new neural pathway to develop in our brain and support us in mastering a new skill. It is also estimated that it takes three to six months to develop that new habit if practiced regularly. Each of our brains is different and may perform somewhat differently. These averages are important to keep in mind.

When thinking about achieving new ways of living without stress, these statistics on new habit creation might feel self-defeating. The good news is that by understanding the science behind behavior change, we can be highly successful. In summary, by being aware, intentional, and focused on developing and executing new behaviors, we can change our patterns of behavior and create new neural pathways in our brains. You can do this successfully by tapping into your senses to express how you feel about making a change, what it will look like, envisioning your future, and connecting it to what is meaningful.

12

MAKE IT WORK FOR YOU

Walk with me into the future. You've been writing with Write to Be Well for several months. You're well versed in the four Write to Be Well steps and have adopted the method as an important part of your lifestyle. It's a habit now. You often start the day with a five-minute check-in to monitor your stress and make a quick plan to organize your day. Sometimes you write for extended periods of time to reflect on the direction your life is taking and whether you're realizing your goals. Like all good habits, the routine of writing is second nature to you now. You enjoy the process and the new awareness your writing exposes. But as may happen with all good habits, a discontent is settling in. You're tired of responding to the same prompts again and again. When this happens, it's time to consider using Write to Be Well in innovative ways so it continues to inspire and motivate you to manage stress and create change. Thanks to the flexibility and scalability of Write to Be Well and its ability to address episodic, acute, and chronic stress, the method will serve you for a lifetime. It is easily adapted to meet your personal stress management needs so you can continue to live the writing lifestyle! This chapter gives you some options, including additional prompts to keep your writing fresh.

FLEXIBILITY

Write to Be Well is a flexible writing method. It can be modified without losing its effectiveness. The only requisite is that you follow the order of the four steps. Each step builds on the prior step, leading you from naming your stress to committing to do something about it. Beyond that, there are a multitude of options that allow for individual difference. You saw some of the flexibility in the approaches of the people whose stories we included in Section 3. Initially, Logan, Amy, Yvonne, and Warren followed the four-step method until they had learned all the steps. Then they adapted Write to Be Well to suit their needs. These writers successfully tweaked the method as they navigated their way through their stressful situation.

Over the past twenty years, I have taken many liberties with Write to Be Well to keep my writing fresh and meaningful. When I was in the throes of grieving the decline of my parents, I often wrote a poem for Step One. I discovered I could express the depth of my feelings better through poetry, even though I'm not a poet, than I could by writing prose. Then, when I got all my feelings down on paper, I could move on to the next steps, which usually ended with an action to advocate on their behalf.

SCALABILITY

Write to Be Well also scales up or down to fit the size of your stress. Jeremy found it worked well with his big issue and all of its little components. He suffered from a digestive disorder that perplexed all the doctors he consulted, yet he was determined to get to the bottom of it. He started using Write to Be Well to see if he could uncover the emotional issues that might be contributing to his distress. In Step One, he named his stress and linked it to his emotions. He repeated the step again and again, discovering many layers of contributing factors rooted in his childhood. He then took these concerns to his therapist for further analysis. By consistently working with the big issue, Jeremy broke it down into smaller pieces that he was able to tackle one at a time. Scaling Write to Be Well helped Jeremy attend to all the details of his discomfort—big and small—and finally resolve the issue that had plagued him for years.

The time spent with Write to Be Well can also be scaled. You decide whether you want to spend sixty minutes writing in one sitting or write in four fifteen-minute segments or less when you have time constraints. Depending on what's going on in your life, you decide if you want to repeat one step many times before completing the remaining steps or complete all four steps in rapid succession. Once you settle into the basic approach, you simply go with what you need in the current moment. Your writing empowers you to be in charge of your life rather than a victim of the stress and emotion that can overwhelm you.

Sam, just one person among many who uses Write to Be Well regularly, recently started working for a new company. During his fourth week on the job, he was stressed out about office personalities and politics. Rather than getting embroiled in what was going on in the office, he decided to write about it. He responded to Step One in fifteen-minute increments each day for the whole week, using his journal to unload his stress. Over the weekend, after reflecting on what he wrote, he spent less than an hour writing about his values before crafting a clear affirmation and goal. Then he listed the actions he was going to take to deal with his stress. In his journal, he wrote, *Writing with Write to Be Well is like having a multifunction stress management tool in my pocket. The time I spend with it is totally up to me.*

Big problem or little problem, short time or expansive time—Write to Be Well adapts well in all situations.

ACUTE OR CHRONIC STRESS

Thanks to the flexibility and scalability of Write to Be Well, you can also tackle acute or chronic stress with this method. Acute stress, which may arise from something as simple as choosing the wrong line at the grocery or getting stuck in traffic, may get your blood boiling, especially if you're in a hurry. Or you may find your stress escalating quickly, as I did after receiving an unfavorable health diagnosis. Stress tends to intensify over time, magnifying the initial discomfort and creating fears of the consequences. When this happens, you can stop the uneasiness created by acute stress by writing about it. Clients have told us they've written the four steps on a paper napkin while sitting in a coffeehouse; others have started a journal that now has pages and pages of writing. Joanie says she writes in the doctor's waiting room before she has her blood-pressure test. She says it calms her down.

Unlike acute stress, *chronic* stress plagues us over extended periods of time. Parents often find themselves trying to juggle a busy work schedule along with finances and the constant demands of childcare. Students are challenged by unexpectedly heavy workloads or impending exams. Healthcare patients struggle with weight issues, chronic illnesses, and a myriad of other health problems. The constant stressors can add to existing health problems or create new ones, bringing additional sources of physical and emotional discomfort. Writing about your chronic stress transfers your pain to your journal. Once you name it, you have a better chance of managing it. Dustin writes to manage the intense stress he experiences when he reads the newspaper. He says he likes to keep up with world events but becomes so distressed that he can feel his anger mounting. When he writes, he gets all those pent-up feelings on paper, releasing the steam he feels building inside him.

The beauty of Write to Be Well is that it can be tailored to address your stress also. Use it once in an acute situation or over time to manage chronic conditions.

HOW TO KEEP YOUR WRITING GOING OVER TIME

Variety is said to be the spice of life! To keep your writing interesting, consider these suggestions.

Join a Writing Support Group

When your stress feels overwhelming or you begin to isolate by withdrawing from friends and family, it may be time to join a writing support group. Sharing your experiences with other people who are also living with stress, even if their stress is different from yours, changes the loneliness dynamic by putting you in relationship with others who will bear witness to your story, as you will to theirs. In a group, you are more than a person brooding in isolation about your stress; you are a companion on the journey of life, sharing the joy and pain we can all understand

and appreciate. With writing as your common bond, your group will share personal stories, challenges, and triumphs. They will hear your individual testimony and validate the meaning you give to your experience. Empathetic listeners care about our stories. They reinforce our belief in ourselves and encourage us to change our situation by making difficult lifestyle choices.

There are hundreds of writing groups. A quick search of the internet reveals a variety of approaches, from creative writing to therapeutic writing. Some are led by professionals, such as mental health therapists or social workers; others are self-led, with group members sharing the leadership role. It's important to find a group that's right for you. Creative writing focuses on the creative process, whereas therapeutic writing is about self-discovery, telling your stories, and healing. So if your goal is to address your stress, make behavior changes, or heal emotional trauma, you may do better with a therapeutic writing group that is run by a professional. Your leader could be a healthcare professional or a writing instructor trained and certified in Write to Be Well or other healing writing modalities. These professionals create safe spaces where privacy and confidentiality are honored. You'll find therapeutic writing groups in hospitals, cancer centers, therapist offices, and community centers. Ask your healthcare provider for a referral or check the credentials of your workshop leader.

You may also discover virtual writing groups online, where members are known only by first name. Check out our website, www. thegetwellproject.com, for an online Write to Be Well group and to find links to other writing group resources across the internet.

Find a Writing Buddy

Another way to add variety to your writing journey is to find a writing companion by partnering with a spouse or friend.

Husband and wife Sharone and Jamel agreed to write together to manage their stress around his rising blood pressure. Their story is an example of how Write to Be Well can be adapted to couples, families, and friends who share health concerns. Although Jamel is the identified "patient," Sharone's fears about his health increase her stress. By writing together, they share their worries and find ways to support each other in their wellness journeys. Sharone writes,

When Jamel's blood pressure started inching up, I knew he was in trouble. His dad and mom both had high blood pressure. It's in his genes and there's not much he can do about that. When his nurse mentioned writing as a way of controlling stress and changing behavior, I jumped on it! I thought writing might help him commit to an exercise program. I admit, I had to push a bit, especially when he told me, "I don't write!"

Anyway, he agreed as long as I would do it with him. It's really been interesting. The writing helped us identify some fears we share and opened up a difficult discussion about our future. I confessed I was afraid he might end up like his dad, with me having to take care of him. He admitted he was afraid of that too.

What I have loved about writing alongside Jamel is how it opened up some heartfelt discussions. We're both committed now to an exercise program. We're going to do it together. And we know why we're doing it. It's not just to control stress, although that's important; it's also because we value each other and our family. We want to be healthy for them as well as ourselves.

Work with a Therapist, Counselor, Pastor, Coach, or Healthcare Provider

If you're stumped about how to address your stress, you may want to consult a professional to help you unravel the myriad issues and emotions that have you tied up in knots. Write to Be Well is not a substitute for professional psychological or medical care when your writing brings up issues more complex than you can solve by yourself. Instead, a professional, working alongside you, can clarify your options and challenge your thinking. By bouncing your ideas off of another person, you gain fresh insights into your stress and what to do about it. Using Write to Be Well complements professional help. In your journal, you write to deepen your understanding of your stress, your feelings and emotions, and your values. With renewed clarity, you're primed to create a plan for change and realize your goals, all of which can be shared with a professional. Over time, gaining control over your response to stress may very well help you feel better and be healthy. This is the ultimate goal of both professional treatment and Write to Be Well.

In chapter 10, Warren talked with his pastor about his grief following the loss of his wife. He also used Write to Be Well before and after his conversations with the pastor to clarify his thoughts and feelings. He found the writing brought up issues to discuss with the pastor and also helped him reflect on their discussion following a session. The talking and writing worked together to shed light on his understanding of the complex grief he was experiencing.

Vary the Prompts in Write to Be Well

Substituting some of the prompts in each of the four steps helps you approach your issue from a fresh angle and add variety to your writing. Use the ones we suggest here, or sign up for the free offer on our website (www.thegetwellproject.com) to receive "Write to be Well: 30 Prompts to Get Started." Remember, it's important that you follow the sequence of the four-step method. Each step builds on the previous one to deliver powerful results!

Here are some alternative prompts that follow the four-step method. They're guaranteed to spice up your writing and keep you moving toward your goal to manage stress!

Step One: Write Your Stress Story

Step One prompts help you name your stress and link details with emotions.

- Describe your relationship with stress by creating a list for each of these statements: How stress negatively impacts my life. What feels uncomfortable or disturbs me about my stress? The biggest challenges I'm facing now regarding my stress. What gives me hope in the face of this stress?
- If stress were a color, it would be . . . Why? What emotions do you associate with this color? What would be your color without the stress? Why?
- Write a character sketch with your stress as the main character. Describe it as a person, animal, or other living thing. What does stress look like? How does it behave? Who hangs out with stress? How do you feel about living with this stress as part of your life?

- What feels broken in your life right now? Is it a stress you're experiencing? A health issue? An old trauma? A work problem? Describe what's broken, how you feel about it, and why it needs to be fixed.
- Explore the metaphors you use to describe your stress by finishing one of these two sentence stems with a word or image that captures the meaning of stress for you: *Stress is . . . Stress is like a . . .* Read and reflect on what you've written. What surprises you? Does your metaphor help to describe or explain your experience with stress and emotional response to it?
- Draw a horizontal line across your page with hash marks to represent ten-year periods. Mark each decade with your age—10, 20, 30, etc. Now reflect on your life. Where on this time line were there periods of stress? Choose one and let that be your writing topic for Step One. Or mark your horizontal line with hours of the day. What happened today or yesterday to increase your stress? Is this a pattern in your day? Include details and link your details with your emotions.

Step Two: Affirm Your Stressless Future

Step Two prompts help you envision a future where you're managing your stress and living according to your values.

- Who would you be if you didn't have your current stress? Write from the first-person point of view, starting with "I am . . ." What are you doing and how do you look and feel? What would your typical day look like? How are you managing your stress? Notice yourself from physical, emotional, and spiritual points of view.
- Create a dialogue between your current self and your ideal self. What do they have to say to each other? Read what you've written and reflect on the wisdom of each self as well as the discrepancy in their views. Which case is stronger? What do you want to do now?
- What is the story you want to create for yourself this year? What do you want to say yes to?
- Imagine yourself standing at the top of a mountain of stress you've just climbed. You won the race. What does it look like from up there? How do you feel?

Step Three: Plan to Unravel Stress

Step Three prompts help you formulate your action plan with SMART goals.

- Respond to these sentence stems: *I want to change . . . I want to overcome . . . Life is better when . . . This is what I'm going to do . . .* Create a SMART goal based on what you're going to do.
- Will you let your stress define you or rule your life? If yes, why is this acceptable to you? If not, what are you willing to do about it? Be specific in listing what you will do and then create a SMART goal.
- Write about "holding on" and "letting go." What are you having trouble holding on to or letting go of? Have you cleaned out the "stuff" of life to embrace a new beginning? What will you do now? Create a SMART goal.
- What do you need to do to get your life untangled and move forward with renewed vitality? List the steps you plan to take. Write a SMART goal for your first step.
- What resources and help would you like or need to propel you toward a healthier you? Do you have these supports in your life? If not, how can you engage them? Write a SMART goal to get started.
- Every journey begins with a single step. What's your first step in reducing your stress? Turn it into a SMART goal.

Step Four: Reflect and Commit to Destress

In Step Four prompts, you're asked to reflect on all you've written in the previous three steps and then make a commitment to destress. The following alternative prompts pose questions to deepen your understanding of your life experiences:

- Reflect on difficult periods or events you've navigated in your life. How did you overcome them? Who or what helped you? What did you learn from the experience?
- Write a dialogue between yourself and a family member or friend about what you're learning about yourself in this change process.
- Look at yourself in the mirror. What do you see? Show some compassion for yourself, as you might show a friend in a similar

situation. Write some positive self-talk, complimenting yourself on your gifts and talents and any other wonderful things about you that contribute to your efforts to change a behavior.

- Imagine yourself one year from now. Have you made lifestyle changes? If so, what changes have you made? If not, what has prevented you from making the changes? No matter where you are on the continuum of change, take a moment to praise yourself for what you have done. Then recommit to the change you desire.
- Each of us are the heroes in our own stories. Describe one of your heroic acts. How does it make you feel? What did you learn from it?
- What does commitment mean to you? Are you ready to commit to making lifestyle changes?
- How does your faith sustain you during times of challenge?

WHAT'S NEXT?

We've both been using Write to Be Well for over twenty years. It's second nature to us to write when we want to identify and manage stressful life situations. We may write by jotting down a few notes at the beginning of the day to help us set priorities, thereby avoiding stress. Other times, we'll fill our journals by writing for six months straight, tackling one issue at a time. Then we may skip a few months of writing before coming back to it again. Life has its ebb and flow. What works today may not work tomorrow. Like you, we are a work in progress—always growing and changing, setting new goals and forming new habits. It's what keeps life interesting!

We've found that establishing a consistent writing practice increases our chances of success. It will work for you too! Merely naming your stress gets you unstuck from the negative stuff that can drag you down, putting you on a positive trajectory for change. Then, when you set your goals, you experience the energizing momentum that comes with knowing where you're going and what you're doing about it. This intersection between knowing and doing is the point of awareness—you're more aware of yourself and the inner qualities that will sustain the change you desire.

Setting and meeting your goals builds self-confidence. With each goal met, you feel better about yourself. You know, down to your bones, that you did it once and can do it again. Change is not a one-shot deal. You're not going to shed twenty pounds or confront your stress or achieve the state of wellness you desire in one fell swoop. There are multiple steps you'll need to take to turn your dreams into reality. Write to Be Well will keep you on course. When you write about your stumbling blocks and act on your goals, you engage in conscious self-creation. You choose your life, rather than have it thrust on you. With writing, you can check in on your life and tweak the outcomes as needed.

We invite you to try Write to Be Well. See if it works for you. There is no "one-size-fits-all" answer to stress management. Research validates writing as a wellness modality. It's effective on its own or when used with other traditional stress management tools. You can write anytime, anywhere, as long as you have a pen and a scrap of paper. It's that portable! Enjoy the journey, and go for it!

NOTES

I. STRESS

1. American Diabetes Association, "Stress," accessed March 29, 2018, http://www.diabetes.org/living-with-diabetes/complications/mental-health/stress.html.

2. Theodore M. Brown and Elizabeth Fee, "Walter Bradford Cannon—Pioneer Physiologist of Human Emotions," *American Journal of Public Health* 92, no. 10 (2002): 1594–95.

3. Walter Bradford Cannon, *Bodily Changes in Pain, Hunger, Fear and Rage* (New York: D. Appleton, 1915).

4. Salim Ranabir and K. Reetu, "Stress and Hormones," *Indian Journal of Endocrinology and Metabolism* 15, no. 1 (January–March 2011): 18–22, https://www.ncbi.nlm.nih.gov/pmc/articles/PMC3079864/, doi:10.4103/2230-8210.77573.

5. Brian Luke Seaward, *Managing Stress*, 9th ed. (Burlington, MA: Jones & Bartlett Learning, 2017), 44–57.

6. S. A. McLeod, "What Is the Stress Response," Simply Psychology, https://www.simplypsychology.org/stress-biology.html.

7. Seaward, *Managing Stress*, 61.

8. S. A McLeod, "Stress and Life Events," Simply Psychology, https://www.simplypsychology.org/SRRS.html.

9. Hans Selye, *The Stress of Life* (New York: McGraw-Hill, 1956).

10. Robert M. Sapolsky, *Why Zebras Don't Get Ulcers* (New York: W. H. Freeman, 2009), 1–18.

11. Lindsay Holmes, "10 Weird Signs You Are Stressed Out: Your Body Might Be Trying to Tell You Something," *Huffington Post*, July 24, 2017,

https://www.huffpost.com/entry/weird-signs-youre-stressed-out_n_59721fd8e4b00e4363df16f5.

12. American Psychological Association, "Stress in America: The State of Our Nation," November 1, 2017, 1–8, https://www.apa.org/news/press/releases/stress/2017/state-nation.pdf.

13. Richard Lazarus, *Psychological Stress and the Coping Process* (New York: McGraw-Hill, 1966), 72–99.

14. Seaward, *Managing Stress*, 2–6, 8–10.

15. National Institute of Mental Health, "5 Things You Should Know about Stress," https://www.nimh.nih.gov/health/publications/stress/index.shtml.

16. American Psychological Association, "Stress in America: The State of Our Nation," 1–8.

17. Neil Schneiderman, Gail Ironson, and Scott D. Siegel, "Stress and Health: Psychological, Behavioral, and Biological Determinants," *Annual Review of Clinical Psychology* 1 (November 2004): 607–28.

18. World Health Organization, "Top Ten Causes of Death," May 24, 2018, http://www.who.int/en/news-room/fact-sheets/detail/the-top-10-causes-of-death.

19. International Society for Traumatic Stress Studies, "What Is Traumatic Stress?," http://www.istss.org/public-resources/what-is-traumatic-stress.aspx.

20. Bessel van der Kolk, *The Body Keeps the Score* (New York: Penguin, 2015): 1–88.

21. National Center for PTSD, "How Common Is PTSD?," U.S. Department of Veterans Affairs, https://www.ptsd.va.gov/understand/common/.

22. T. H. Holmes and R. H. Rahe, "The Social Readjustment Rating Scale," *Journal of Psychosomatic Research* 11, no. 2 (August 1967): 213–18.

23. McLeod, "Stress and Life Events."

24. A. D. Kanner, J. C. Coyne, C. Schaefer, and R. S. Lazarus, "Comparison of Two Modes of Stress Measurement: Daily Hassles and Uplifts versus Major Life Events," *Journal of Behavioral Medicine* 4, no. 1 (March 1981): 1–39.

25. Schneiderman, Ironson, and Siegel, "Stress and Health."

26. Jennifer Betts, "Historical Divorce Rate Statistics," Love to Know, https://divorce.lovetoknow.com/Historical_Divorce_Rate_Statistics.

27. American Psychological Association, "Marriage and Divorce," http://www.apa.org/topics/divorce/.

28. Holmes and Rahe, "Social Readjustment Rating Scale," 213–18.

29. Wellness Council of America, "Dr. Brian Luke Seaward: Super Stress Super Storm," https://www.welcoa.org/resources/expert-interview-dr-luke-seaward-super-stress-super-storm/.

30. American Psychological Association, "Marriage and Divorce."

31. Harvard T. H. Chan School of Public Health, "NPR/RWJF/HSPH Poll Finds Health Most Common Major Stressful Event in Americans' Lives Last Year," July 7, 2014, https://www.hsph.harvard.edu/news/press-releases/npr-rwjf-hsph-poll-finds-health-a-common-source-of-stress/.

32. American Institute of Stress, "Workplace Stress," https://www.stress.org/workplace-stress/.

33. American Psychological Association, "Stress in America: Coping with Change," February 15, 2017, https://www.apa.org/news/press/releases/stress/2016/coping-with-change.pdf.

34. American Psychological Association, "Stress in America: The State of Our Nation."

35. Everyday Health, "Exercise and Stress Relief," https://www.everydayhealth.com/exercise-photos/exercises-that-relieve-stress.aspx.

36. Brian Luke Seaward, "Stress and the Human Spirit," May 31, 2009, http://www.brianlukeseaward.com/stress-and-the-human-spirit/.

2. WRITING

1. Louise DeSalvo, *Writing as a Way of Healing: How Telling Our Stories Transforms Our Lives* (Boston: Beacon Press, 2000), 3.

2. DeSalvo, *Writing as a Way of Healing*, 7.

3. DeSalvo, *Writing as a Way of Healing*, 8.

4. DeSalvo, *Writing as a Way of Healing*, 4.

5. Goodreads, "Anais Nin Quotes," https://www.goodreads.com/quotes/tag/anais-nin.

6. J. W. Pennebaker and Joshua M. Smyth, *Opening Up by Writing It Down: How Expressive Writing Improves Health and Eases Emotional Pain* (New York: Guilford Press, 2016), 25.

7. J. W. Pennebaker, *Opening Up: The Healing Power of Expressing Emotions* (New York: Guilford Press, 1990), 26–42.

8. Pennebaker, *Opening Up*, 12–25.

9. Pennebaker, *Opening Up*, 27–29.

10. Pennebaker, *Opening Up*, 34.

11. Gina Roberts-Grey, "Keeping Secrets Can Be Hazardous to Your Health," *Forbes*, October 24, 2013, https://www.forbes.com/sites/nextavenue/2013/10/24/keeping-secrets-can-be-hazardous-to-your-health/#3b6ba72660bd.

12. Pennebaker, *Opening Up*, 2.

13. J. W. Pennebaker, Janice K. Kiecolt-Glaser, and Ronald Glaser, "Disclosure of Traumas and Immune Function: Health Implications for Psychotherapy," *Journal of Consulting and Clinical Psychology* 56, no. 2 (1988): 242.

14. Joshua M. Smyth, Arthur A. Stone, Adam Hurewitz, and Alan Kaell, "Effects of Writing about Stressful Experiences on Symptom Reduction in Patients with Asthma or Rheumatoid Arthritis," *Journal of the American Medical Association* 281, no. 14 (April 14, 1999): 1307.

15. Lynn Willmott et al., "The Effects of Expressive Writing following First Myocardial Infarction: A Randomized Controlled Trial," *Health Psychology* 30, no. 5 (September 2011): 642–50, http://dx.doi.org/10.1037/a0023519.

16. Heidi E. Koschwanez et al., "Expressive Writing and Wound Healing in Older Adults: A Randomized Controlled Trial," *Psychosomatic Medicine* 75, no. 6 (July/August 2013): 581–90, http://dx.doi.org/10.1097/PSY.0b013e31829b7b2e.

17. M. S. Cepeda et al., "Emotional Disclosure through Patient Narrative May Improve Pain and Well-Being: Results of a Randomized Controlled Trial in Patients with Cancer Pain," *Journal of Pain and Symptom Management* 35, no. 6 (June 2008): 623, http://dx.doi.org/10.1016/j.jpainsymman.2007.08.011.

18. Pennebaker and Smyth, *Opening Up by Writing It Down*, 47.

19. Pennebaker and Smyth, *Opening Up by Writing It Down*, 169.

20. Pennebaker and Smyth, *Opening Up by Writing It Down*, 64.

21. Pennebaker and Smyth, *Opening Up by Writing It Down*, 151.

22. Social Psychology Network, "Claude Steele," March 16, 2016, http://Steele.socialpsychology.org/; David K. Sherman and Geoffrey L. Cohen, "The Psychology of Self-Defense: Self-Affirmation Theory," *Advances in Experimental Social Psychology* 38 (2006): 183–242, https://ed.stanford.edu/sites/default/files/self_defense.pdf.

23. David K. Sherman and Geoffrey L. Cohen, "Accepting Threatening Information: Self-Affirmation and the Reduction of Defensive Biases," *Current Directions in Psychological Science* 11, no. 4 (2002): 119–23.

24. Guido M. van Koningsbruggen and Enny Das, "Don't Derogate This Message! Self-Affirmation Promotes Online Type 2 Diabetes Risk Test Taking," *Psychology & Health* 24, no. 6 (2009): 635–49, doi:10.1080/08870440802340156.

25. Tracy Epton and Peter Richard Harris, "Self-Affirmation Promotes Health Behavior Change," *Health Psychology* 27, no. 6 (November 2008): 746–52, doi:10.1037/hea0000116.

26. Ray Williams, "Do Self-Affirmations Work? A Revisit," *Psychology Today*, May 5, 2013, http://www.psychologytoday.com/blog/wired-success/201305/do-self-affirmations-work-revisit.

27. Brian Alger, "Transformative Writing 4: The Secret Life of Words," *Art of Transformative Writing*, April 10, 2016, http://brianalger.com/transformative-writing-secret-life-words/.

28. Edwin A. Locke and Gary P. Latham, "New Directions in Goal Setting Theory," *Current Direction in Psychological Science* 15, no. 5 (October 2006): 265–68.

29. John B. Miner, *Organizational Behavior 1: Essential Theories of Motivation and Leadership* (London: Routledge, 2015), 297–341.

30. Wanderlust Worker, "The Harvard MBA Business School Study on Goal Setting," https://www.wanderlustworker.com/the-harvard-mba-business-school-study-on-goal-setting/.

31. Henriette Anne Klauser, *Write It Down, Make It Happen* (New York: Simon & Schuster, 2000), 31–34.

32. Pennebaker and Smyth, *Opening Up by Writing It Down*, 151.

33. Jeannie Wright and Gillie Bolten, *Reflective Writing in Counselling and Psychotherapy* (London: Sage, 2012), xi.

34. Robert J. Yinger and Christopher M. Clark, "Reflective Journal Writing: Theory and Practice," July 1981, https://eric.ed.gov/?id=ED208411.

35. Pennebaker and Smyth, *Opening Up by Writing It Down*, 135.

36. BrainyQuote, "Wayne Dyer Quotes," https://www.brainyquote.com/authors/wayne_dyer.

37. Sherry Reiter, "What Is Transformative Writing?," Creative Righting Center, May 2, 2016, http://sherryreiter.blogspot.com/2016/05/transformative-writing.html.

4. YOUR FUTURE

1. D. Powell and the Institute of Noetic Sciences, *The 2007 Shift Report: Evidence of a World Transforming* (Petaluma, CA: Institute of Noetic Sciences, 2007): 28–36.

6. YOUR LIFE

1. BrainyQuote, "Wayne Dyer Quotes," https://www.brainyquote.com/authors/wayne_dyer.

8. SINGLE-PARENT JUGGLE

1. J. W. Pennebaker, *Opening Up: The Healing Power of Expressing Emotions* (New York: Guilford Press, 1990), 9.

2. Edwin A. Locke and Gary P. Latham, "New Directions in Goal Setting Theory," *Current Directions in Psychological Science* 15, no. 5 (October 2006): 38.

STAY WELL

1. QuoteFancy, "Tony Robbins Quote," https://quotefancy.com/quote/ 922520/Tony-Robbins-Change-happens-when-the-pain-of-staying-the-same- is-greater-than-the-pain-of.

2. Goodreads, "Anais Nin Quotes," https://www.goodreads.com/author/ quotes/7190.Ana_s_Nin.

3. Simon Sinek, "Commit>Find Your Why," https://startwithwhy.com/ find-your-why/.

11. BUILD YOUR HABIT WITH INTENTION

1. Patrick Zeis, "History's Most Influential Psychologists," Balanced Achievement, March 1, 2018, https://balancedachievement.com/psychology/ influential-psychologists/.

2. William Bridges, *Transitions: Making Sense of Life's Changes* (Cambridge, MA: Perseus Books Group, 2004), 101–76.

3. Goodreads, "The Writing Life Quotes," https://www.goodreads.com/ work/quotes/516929-the-writing-life.

4. BrainyQuote, "Christopher Reeve Quotes," https://www.brainyquote. com/authors/christopher_reeve.

5. Charles Duhigg, *The Power of Habit* (New York: Random House, 2012) 60–93.

BIBLIOGRAPHY

Alger, Brian. "Transformative Writing 4: The Secret Life of Words." *Art of Transformative Writing*, April 10, 2016. http://brianalger.com/transformative-writing-secret-life-words/.

American Diabetes Association. "Stress." Accessed March 29, 2018. http://www.diabetes.org/living-with-diabetes/complications/mental-health/stress.html.

American Institute of Stress. "Workplace Stress." https://www.stress.org/workplace-stress/.

American Psychological Association. "Marriage and Divorce." http://www.apa.org/topics/divorce/.

———. "Stress in America: Coping with Change." February 15, 2017. https://www.apa.org/news/press/releases/stress/2016/coping-with-change.pdf.

———. "Stress in America: The State of Our Nation." November 1, 2017. https://www.apa.org/news/press/releases/stress/2017/state-nation.pdf.

Betts, Jennifer. "Historical Divorce Rate Statistics." Love to Know. https://divorce.lovetoknow.com/Historical_Divorce_Rate_Statistics.

BrainyQuote. "Christopher Reeve Quotes." https://www.brainyquote.com/authors/christopher_reeve.

———. "Wayne Dyer Quotes." https://www.brainyquote.com/authors/wayne_dyer.

Bridges, William. *Transitions: Making Sense of Life's Changes*. Cambridge, MA: Perseus Books Group, 2004.

Brown, Theodore M., and Elizabeth Fee. "Walter Bradford Cannon—Pioneer Physiologist of Human Emotions." *American Journal of Public Health*, 92, no. 10 (2002): 1594–95.

Cannon, Walter Bradford. *Bodily Changes in Pain, Hunger, Fear and Rage*. New York: D. Appleton, 1915.

Cepeda, M. S., et al. "Emotional Disclosure through Patient Narrative May Improve Pain and Well-Being: Results of a Randomized Controlled Trial in Patients with Cancer Pain." *Journal of Pain and Symptom Management* 35, no. 6 (June 2008): 623–31. https://doi.org/10.1016/j.jpainsymman.2007.08.011.

DeSalvo, Louise. *Writing as a Way of Healing: How Telling Our Stories Transforms Our Lives*. Boston: Beacon Press, 2000.

Duhigg, Charles. *The Power of Habit*. New York: Random House, 2012.

Epton, Tracy, and Peter Richard Harris. "Self-Affirmation Promotes Health Behavior Change." *Health Psychology* 27, no. 6 (November 2008): 746–52. doi:10.1037/hea0000116.

Everyday Health. "Exercise and Stress Relief." https://www.everydayhealth.com/exercise-photos/exercises-that-relieve-stress.aspx.

Goodreads. "Anais Nin Quotes." https://www.goodreads.com/quotes/tag/anais-nin.

———. "The Writing Life Quotes." https://www.goodreads.com/work/quotes/516929-the-writing-life.

Harvard T. H. Chan School of Public Health. "NPR/RWJF/HSPH Poll Finds Health Most Common Major Stressful Event in Americans' Lives Last Year." July 7, 2014. https://www.hsph.harvard.edu/news/press-releases/npr-rwjf-hsph-poll-finds-health-a-common-source-of-stress/.

Holmes, Lindsay. "10 Weird Signs You Are Stressed Out." *Huffington Post*, July 24, 2017. https://www.huffpost.com/entry/weird-signs-youre-stressed-out_n_59721fd8e4b00e4363df16f5.

Holmes, T. H., and R. H. Rahe. "The Social Readjustment Rating Scale." *Journal of Psychosomatic Research* 11, no. 2 (August 1967): 213–18.

International Society for Traumatic Stress Studies. "What Is Traumatic Stress?" http://www.istss.org/public-resources/what-is-traumatic-stress.aspx.

Kanner, A. D., J. C. Coyne, C. Schaefer, and R. S. Lazarus. "Comparison of Two Modes of Stress Measurement: Daily Hassles and Uplifts versus Major Life Events." *Journal of Behavioral Medicine* 4, no. 1 (March 1981): 1–39.

Klauser, Henriette Anne. *Write It Down, Make It Happen*. New York: Simon & Schuster, 2000.

Koschwanez, Heidi E., et al. "Expressive Writing and Wound Healing in Older Adults: A Randomized Controlled Trial." *Psychosomatic Medicine* 75, no. 6 (July/August 2013): 581–90. https://doi.org/10.1097/PSY.0b013e31829b7b2e.

Lazarus, Richard. *Psychological Stress and the Coping Process*. New York: McGraw-Hill, 1966.

Locke, Edwin A., and Gary P. Latham. "New Directions in Goal Setting Theory." *Current Directions in Psychological Science* 15, no. 5 (October 2006): 265–68.

McLeod, S. A. "Biology of Stress Introduction." Simply Psychology. https://www.simplypsychology.org/SRRS.html.

———. "Stress and Life Events." Simply Psychology. 2010. https://www.simplypsychology.org/SRRS.html.

Miner, John B. *Organizational Behavior 1: Essential Theories of Motivation and Leadership*. London: Routledge, 2015.

National Center for PTSD. "How Common Is PTSD?" U.S. Department of Veterans Affairs. https://www.ptsd.va.gov/understand/common/.

National Institute of Mental Health. "5 Things You Should Know about Stress." https://www.nimh.nih.gov/health/publications/stress/index.shtml.

Pennebaker, James W. *Opening Up: The Healing Power of Expressing Emotions*. New York: Guilford Press, 1990.

Pennebaker, James W., Janice K. Kiecolt-Glaser, and Ronald Glaser. "Disclosure of Traumas and Immune Function: Health Implications for Psychotherapy." *Journal of Consulting and Clinical Psychology* 56, no. 2 (1988): 239–45.

Pennebaker, James W., and Joshua M. Smyth. *Opening Up by Writing It Down: How Expressive Writing Improves Health and Eases Emotional Pain*. New York: Guilford Press, 2016.

Powell, D., and the Institute of Noetic Sciences. *The 2007 Shift Report: Evidence of a World Transforming*. Petaluma, CA: Institute of Noetic Sciences, 2007.

QuoteFancy. "Tony Robbins Quote." https://quotefancy.com/quote/922520/Tony-Robbins-Change-happens-when-the-pain-of-staying-the-same-is-greater-than-the-pain-of.

Ranabir, Salim, and K. Reetu. "Stress and Hormones." *Indian Journal of Endocrinology and Metabolism* 15, no. 1 (January–March 2011): 18–22. https://www.ncbi.nlm.nih.gov/pmc/articles/PMC3079864/. doi:10.4103/2230-8210.77573.

Reiter, Sherry. "What Is Transformative Writing?" Creative Righting Center, May 2, 2016. http://sherryreiter.blogspot.com/2016/05/transformative-writing.html.

Roberts-Grey, Gina. "Keeping Secrets Can Be Hazardous to Your Health." *Forbes*, October 24, 2013. https://www.forbes.com/sites/nextavenue/2013/10/24/keeping-secrets-can-be-hazardous-to-your-health/#63bb4b6060bd.

Sapolsky, Robert M. *Why Zebras Don't Get Ulcers*. New York: W. H. Freeman, 2009.

Schneiderman, Neil, Gail Ironson, and Scott D. Siegel. "Stress and Health: Psychological, Behavioral, and Biological Determinants." *Annual Review of Clinical Psychology* 1 (November 2004): 607–28.

Seaward, Brian Luke. *Managing Stress.* 9th ed. Burlington, MA: Jones & Bartlett Learning, 2017.

———. "Stress and the Human Spirit." May 31, 2009. http://www.brianlukeseaward.com/stress-and-the-human-spirit/.

Selye, Hans. *The Stress of Life.* New York: McGraw-Hill, 1956.

Sherman, David K., and Geoffrey L. Cohen. "Accepting Threatening Information: Self-Affirmation and the Reduction of Defensive Biases." *Current Directions in Psychological Science* 11, no. 4 (2002): 119–23.

———. "The Psychology of Self-Defense: Self-Affirmation Theory." *Advances in Experimental Social Psychology* 38 (2006): 183–242.

Sinek, Simon. "Commit>Find Your Why." https://startwithwhy.com/find-your-why/.

Smyth, Joshua M., Arthur A. Stone, Adam Hurewitz, and Alan Kaell. "Effects of Writing about Stressful Experiences on Symptom Reduction in Patients with Asthma or Rheumatoid Arthritis." *Journal of the American Medical Association* 281, no. 14 (April 14, 1999): 1304–9.

Social Psychology Network. "Claude Steele." http://Steele.socialpsychology.org/.

van der Kolk, Bessel. *The Body Keeps the Score.* New York: Penguin, 2015.

van Koningsbruggen, Guido M., and Enny Das. "Don't Derogate This Message! Self-Affirmation Promotes Online Type 2 Diabetes Test Taking." *Psychology & Health* 24, no. 6 (2009): 635–49. https://doi.org/10.1080/08870440802340156.

Wanderlust Worker. "The Harvard MBA Business School Study on Goal Setting." https://www.wanderlustworker.com/the-harvard-mba-business-school-study-on-goal-setting/.

Wellness Council of America. "Dr. Brian Luke Seaward Super Stress Super Storm." https://www.welcoa.org/resources/expert-interview-dr-luke-seaward-super-stress-super-storm/.

Williams, Ray. "Do Self-Affirmations Work? A Revisit." *Psychology Today*, May 5, 2013. https://www.psychologytoday.com/blog/wired-success/201305/do-self-affirmations-work-revisit.

Willmott, L., et al. "The Effects of Expressive Writing following First Myocardial Infarction: A Randomized Controlled Trial." *Health Psychology* 30, no. 5 (2011): 642–50. http://dx.doi.org/10.1037/a0023519.

World Health Organization. "Top Ten Causes of Death." May 24, 2018. http://www.who.int/en/news-room/fact-sheets/detail/the-top-10-causes-of-death.

Wright, Jeannie, and Gillie Bolten. *Reflective Writing in Counselling and Psychotherapy.* London: Sage, 2012.

Yinger, Robert J., and Christopher M. Clark. "Reflective Journal Writing: Theory and Practice." July 1981. https://eric.ed.gov/?id=ED208411.

Zeis, Patrick. "History's Most Influential Psychologists." Balanced Achievement, March 1, 2018. https://balancedachievement.com/psychology/influential-psychologists/.

ACKNOWLEDGMENTS

Our profound thanks to all the people who supported us on this three-year journey from proposal writing to finished manuscript: Claire Gerus, our literary agent, who believed in our book idea, and we couldn't have done it without her; Kay Adams, Deborah Ross, and John Evans, who believed in our concept and endorsed our proposal; Ann Paciulli, Dr. Mark Cooper, and Lisa Colburn, for their feedback through fresh eyes and careful reading of the draft manuscript; the people whose stories enliven these pages by courageously agreeing to share their writing experiences with Write to Be Well; and our publisher, for believing in us as first-time authors.

DIANE HARTINGH PRICE

With a grateful heart, I am filled with thanks to so many along this journey of learning and creativity! My loving thanks to my lifelong friend and coauthor, Sue McCollum, for our steadfast friendship, sharing her writing expertise, and helping me to focus on detail—ever a challenge through my big-picture lens. Loving thanks to my family and friends for their support, ongoing interest, and encouragement. A special thank-you to my loving husband, Nelson, for his support, patience, and ongoing encouragement.

SUSAN IVES McCOLLUM

My biggest thank-you to Diane Price, my coauthor and dear friend, who guided me over the rough patches when I got bogged down in a jumble of words. Her clarity and big-picture vision kept us on target. Thanks also to my family, near and far, who provided emotional support and encouragement by asking, "How's it going?"; to Mary Tuchscherer, who gave me the opportunity of a lifetime to lead women's writing groups internationally with VoiceFlame; to my friends at Goose Creek Friends Meeting and from other walks of life, who graciously agreed to use the writing method and provide feedback; and to my writing group, my companions on the way, for their belief in me as a writer and writing facilitator. My enduring love and gratitude to my husband, Doug, who opened up space for my writing by doing laundry, dishes, errands, and a myriad of other tasks that keep a home running smoothly. His encouragement and dinners out kept me going and well fed.

INDEX

achievable, as SMART goal, 68, 69–70, 105, 122, 128, 130, 143, 148, 173, 177

acknowledgment, with Endings stage, 185

action plan, 67; guidelines for, 71; key elements of, 74; prompts for, 72–73; reflection on, 74; SMART goals for, 31–32, 32, 34, 67–71, 72, 74, 198–203; to unravel stress, 72. *See also specific action plans*

action scripting, 21, 37, 67; goal-setting theories relating to, 32; Larry relating to, 33–34; Locke and Latham research relating to, 32–33, 123; reducing stress challenge of, 31–34; SMART goals, 73, 77–78

acute stress, 8, 10, 10–11, 195; flexibility and scalability of writing with, 197

acute stressors, 16

adaptability, of Write to Be Well, 196, 197

Adler, Alfred, 184, 185

affirmation, of future, 55–56; appropriate language for, 60; guidelines for, 56–58; key elements of, 61; prompts for, 58–60, 92; reflection relating to, 60–61, 92; as stressless, 58–65, 92; tips for, 59–60

affirmations, xi, xiii, 28, 37; of Amy, 118–121, 127, 130; of Diane, xi; of Jason, 29–30; of Logan, 102–104, 111; of Manuel, 29; of Paul, 61–65; of Sue, xiii; positive, 29, 30, 31; self-

affirmation, 29, 30–31; of Warren, 162–164, 172–173, 176, 176–177; of Yvonne, 139–141, 142, 147–148, 150, 153

affirmative writing, 21, 37; confidence in future built by, 27–31; description of, 27–28; family relating to, 64; financial security relating to, 64; integrity relating to, 64; Manuel relating to, 28–29; positive words for, 28, 58, 59–60, 61, 164, 190, 192, 204

aha moment, 1, 2, 40, 82, 182, 184

alteration, of habits, 189

alternative prompts, 201–204

American Institute for Preventive Medicine, 16–17

American Psychological Association, 17, 18

Amy: co-parenting of, 115, 116, 120; professional life of, 115; reflection relating to, 128; as single mother, 115–116; SMART goals for, 122, 123, 126, 127, 128, 129, 130; stress of, 115–116, 117, 121

Amy, action plan created by, 121, 127, 128; commentary of, 123, 129, 130; prompts for, 121–122, 128; reflection relating to, 122–123, 128–129

Amy, affirmation of, 118, 127, 130; commentary of, 120–121; identify what matters, 118–119; prompts for,

ABOUT THE AUTHORS

Diane Hartingh Price is a veteran consultant with more than thirty years' experience and has achieved a reputation for creativity in developing and implementing strategies for helping client organizations achieve change at the intersection of people, process, and technology while growing and operating a profitable business. She worked with public and private organizations in the United States and abroad. In 1994, she began to focus exclusively on working with healthcare organizations. She was certified as an integrative health coach at Duke University's School of Integrative Medicine and completed coursework in "Leading Patients in Writing for Health" for healthcare professionals. Diane lives in Chapel Hill, North Carolina.

Susan Ives McCollum is a psychotherapist and therapeutic writing coach who helps others overcome the stumbling blocks that undermine happiness and fulfillment. She studied therapeutic writing at the Therapeutic Writing Institute, founded by Kathleen Adams, where she discovered the pioneering work of James W. Pennebaker and his impressive scientific data on the physical and emotional benefits of expressive writing. Since then, Sue has led creative writing and memoir workshops for more than ten years, both in the United States and abroad, where she has witnessed the universal healing power of writing, opening writers to life-changing possibilities for optimal health. Sue completed additional coursework with the Therapeutic Writing Institute and Duke University's "Leading Patients in Writing for Health" for healthcare professionals. She lives in Purcellville, Virginia.